OVERCOMING CRISIS

A Spiritual Approach

Idemudia Guobadia

Table of Contents

Acknowledgments and Dedication

It is with a sense of joy and thanksgiving that I solely dedicate this book to JESUS CHRIST, the One that empowered me and gave me the grace to overcome life's crisis. It is only because of Jesus Christ that I never stopped believing that all the crises life threw at me was for my promotion. Lord Jesus Christ, so long as I have breath, I will tell the world about You through writing, preaching, and speaking. I will encourage others that you have endowed with abilities to do same.

I will be remiss if I do not appreciate my beautiful wife, Pastor Tayo Guobadia for her deep patience and under-standing. Tayo, your sacrifices and prayers are incapable of quantification. Thank you for all that you sacrifice to make me a better ambassador for Christ.

I must also acknowledge my wonderful co-laborers in Christ at Overcomers In Christ Group of Churches that continuously demonstrate the love of Christ and make it so delightful for me to serve God in their midst.

Idemudia Guobadia
Union, New Jersey
January 2018

CHAPTER ONE

The Crisis On the Way

The first crisis you had to face and which you had no clue about was your date of birth. You did not plan your birth and, yet you were the main actor in that plot. You survived that crisis because other personalities in the plot unbeknownst to you, were acting on your behalf. That crisis demanded that you leave the familiarity of your mother's womb to a world plagued with all sorts of adversities, intrigues, and crises. The familiarity of your mother's womb was no longer a justification for you to remain in it. You had outgrown the womb of your mother and it was no longer a sufficient environment to nurture you with the abundant life needed for the life journey ahead of you. In similar fashion, many have been limited from breaking into new frontiers of abundant living by the influence of the familiar. Often time, a crisis comes to compel us to move in the direction of progress.

It was the unfolding of adversities and crises that eventually made Job curse the date of his birth (Job 3).

What I feared has come upon me; what I dreaded has happened to me. I have no peace, no quietness; I have no rest, but only turmoil. Job 3:25-26.

The crisis that Job was apprehensive of eventually came to him. Job was a man of substantial means and because of the interplay of divine forces, he lost his wealth and children in the most bizarre manner. The fact that Job was a righteous man that feared God and shunned evil did not prevent him from going through such a gruesome crisis. At the end of the crisis, Job came out stronger, wiser, and richer. God restored unto him that which he had lost and much more. The crisis that Job went through resulted in his promotion and in his experiencing of abundant life of a fuller and richer quality than he previously knew. In the peak of his crisis, Job refused to curse God and die. Rather, Job longed for an opportunity to plead his case and his cause with God.

One character of crisis is its accuracy at testing the heart of man. A crisis will easily show where you stand. Crisis is a good revealer and judge of character. Crisis will show if one is faithful to what he professes or if one has a spirit of compromise. A crisis provokes the real you to come out of the box. Until the real you comes out of hiding, you cannot appreciate the abundant life that Christ came to give.

The crisis of the cross brought Jesus Christ to a crossroad at the Garden of Gethsemane. This crisis demanded that Jesus Christ choose either his will or the will of the Father. As Christ experienced the crisis of the cross, all his followers forsook him and yet, he remained faithful to his Father's will. The crisis of the cross eventually paved way for the glory of Christ's resurrection. In crisis, there will be times that it will seem that you are all alone. You must choose God's will over the fleshly desire to quit or compromise.

From Job 3:25, it appears that Job had a premonition that crisis was coming his way. A crisis can easily arrive at one's doorstep unannounced. Many have this premonition like Job and cannot quite put their fingers to it. We are now in the season of great uncertainties where the abnormal is now seen as normal. Nonetheless, there is a wave of events soon to take place that will catch many unawares. It will be kind of like the famine in Egypt but only that this time around, very few are paying heed to the voice of Joseph.

As the powerful elites of the world clandestinely prepare to usher in a New World Order, a series of intense crises will certainly surround the birthing of this New World Order. It is the toll that this will have on mankind that makes this a crisis like no other in terms of severity of scope and magnitude.

In his earthly ministry, Christ presented two masters before the people: God and Mammon.

No one can serve two masters. Either you will hate the one and love the other, or you will be devoted to the one and despise the other. You cannot serve both God and money. Matthew 6:24.

Financial Crisis

The first wave of crisis that has already been released into the world is a financial crisis of enormous proportions. The United States and many western countries are burdened by an insurmountable debt burden coupled with currencies that are fast depreciating in value. Unemployment rates are rising, and the middle class is on a downward spiral. The world economy is interconnected and so obviously, many countries will be caught in a long term economic recession. All these of course, will influence the speed, the scope, and the depth at which the gospel of Christ will be financed. Those that live a Christ-centered life will experience an inner peace amidst this outward turmoil (John 16:33).

Most churches depend on the contributions of their members. When members are faced with their own financial challenges, it becomes difficult for them to provide regular financial support to their own churches. The church of Christ must ask God for wisdom to navigate through the lean years. Church expenses like mortgage payments, rent, utility bills and insurance premiums will have to be met regardless of fluctuating income. The body of Christ is entering a season where the more affluent members will be expected to carry more of the burden so that the gospel will thrive and prosper. This in turn, will demand more transparency and accountability on the part of serious church leadership. A glimpse of this scenario which is most likely to come to the fore shortly, can be found in Acts Chapters 4 and 5. The Church must adopt a similar approach to remain relevant in this fast-changing world. Without adequate financing the work of the ministry will slow down.

> [32] All the believers were one in heart and mind. No one claimed that any of their possessions was their own, but they shared everything they had. [33] With great power the apostles continued to testify to the resurrection of the Lord Jesus. And God's grace was so powerfully at work in them all [34] that there were no needy persons among them. For from time to time those who owned land or houses sold them, brought the money from the sales [35] and put it at the apostles' feet, and it was distributed to anyone who had need.
>
> [36] Joseph, a Levite from Cyprus, whom the apostles called Barnabas (which means "son of encourage-ment"), [37] sold a field he owned and brought the money and put it at the apostles' feet.
>
> 5. [1]Now a man named Ananias, together with his wife Sapphira, also sold a piece of property. [2] With his wife's full knowledge he kept back part of the money for himself, but brought the rest and put it at the apostles' feet.
>
> [3] Then Peter said, "Ananias, how is it that Satan has so filled your heart that you have lied to the Holy

Spirit and have kept for yourself some of the money you received for the land? [4] Didn't it belong to you before it was sold? And after it was sold, wasn't the money at your disposal? What made you think of doing such a thing? You have not lied just to human beings but to God."

[5] When Ananias heard this, he fell down and died. And great fear seized all who heard what had happened. [6] Then some young men came forward, wrapped up his body, and carried him out and buried him.

[7] About three hours later his wife came in, not knowing what had happened. [8] Peter asked her, "Tell me, is this the price you and Ananias got for the land?"

"Yes," she said, "that is the price."

[9] Peter said to her, "How could you conspire to test the Spirit of the Lord? Listen! The feet of the men who buried your husband are at the door, and they will carry you out also."

[10] At that moment she fell down at his feet and died. Then the young men came in and, finding her dead, carried her out and buried her beside her husband. [11] Great fear seized the whole church and all who heard about these events. Acts 4:32 – Acts 5:11.

Ananias and his wife Sapphira sought to impress the church leaders. They wanted people to think that they were giving to the work of the Lord wholeheartedly. Even though they gave, they were deceptive in their giving. In times of economic hardship, the temptation to be deceptive will increase and we must overcome such temptation. With global financial crisis at the door, the Church will begin to experience new patterns and avenues of giving and must be ready and willing to adapt to changes swiftly.

Generally speaking, the way churches are birthed makes it rather difficult for them to consider merging with a view to consolidating their strengths and minimizing their weaknesses. Churches, though under the same lordship of Jesus Christ, are gifted differently and tend to operate differently. Just like in the European Union where many member states are unwilling to surrender their national sovereignty for the common good, many churches, despite financial challenges, will prefer to work loosely with other churches than to commit to a legal arrangement that will cause a merger of churches. Churches tend to be jealous of their identity, which is often made more complicated by the cluster of denominations and independence within the body of Christ. However, it will not be surprising to see a few church branches within the same denomination and geographical area amalgamate to save operating costs.

Harsh economic realities will most likely result in an increase in crime. With inflation and lack of access to funds, people will get increasingly desperate. The church with an apostolic base and a prophetic voice will of a sudden be in higher demand. People in search of answers will flock to churches where God is speaking. Already, there is a trend with people getting dissatisfied with church as usual. The people that are looking for more of God have been frustrated by the experience of more church, and less God. As financial crisis unfolds, people in desperation will begin to look toward churches that are less talk and more of a demonstration of God's Spirit and power.

Political and Social Crises

Many countries that were created by colonial and other external forces are beginning to fall apart. Many countries were formed in the past century without regard to ethnic, cultural, historical, and religious antecedents. Frictions in these countries along these fault lines have given birth to all manner of security challenges including state sponsored terrorism. The West has also witnessed an intensity in the level of political and social discord within and without her borders. With recent immigration trends, there has been an outcry from western citizens for tighter policing of their countries' borders. The 2015/2016 refugee crisis emanating from ISIS and Syria has seen an influx of Moslem immigrants into Western Europe especially. Many of these Moslem immigrants crossed into the West without any form of documentation or identification. With this, Western Europe has seen an increase in terrorist attacks on her soil.

The US President, Donald Trump has never failed to speak sternly about thoroughly vetting and profiling Moslems in the United States. Since assuming the Presidency, Donald Trump has not deviated from this position. The faith most seem to profess in the United States is still Christianity. The concerns expressed by Mr. Trump may be viewed as recognition of the tensions that exist between Christianity and the Islamic world. What is the Church to do? Is there an Islamic agenda against Christianity?

The concerns of Christians especially regarding the activities of Islamic fundamentalists have not really been satisfactorily addressed by mainstream Moslem leadership. Christians, as well as moderate Moslems, have been the target of persecution at the hands of Islamic fundamentalists and terrorists. Since most Islamic extremists are recruited from the pool of mainstream Islam, many Christians tend to view Islam as pursuing simultaneously, a clandestine and an overt program against the Christian faith. ISIS continues to systematically behead Christians in accordance with their version of Sharia Law. An antichrist spirit is no doubt responsible for the opposition against the Christian faith that we are seeing come from the Moslem world.

> [2] This is how you can recognize the Spirit of God: Every spirit that acknowledges that Jesus Christ has come in the flesh is from God, [3] but every spirit that does not acknowledge Jesus is not from God. This is the spirit of the antichrist, which you have heard is coming and even now is already in the world. 1 John 4:2-3.

The antichrist spirit seeks to take the place of Christ and act as a substitute for Christ. The antichrist is called the beast. He is the leading son of Satan. Islam is packaged as a religion of peace and submission. In Daniel 8:25, we see that by peace, the antichrist shall destroy many and shall oppose Christ. Islam and Christianity are not in agreement on the person, nature, and character of God. By definition, it implies that the spirit of Islam is the spirit of antichrist. Islam is not pro-Christ. Jesus stated that if you are not for him, you are against him (Matthew 12:30).

We should not be surprised to witness an increase in persecution of Christians in areas controlled by Moslems such as the Middle East, Northern Nigeria, Sudan, and Pakistan. As unfortunate as this is, the Christian faith has always spread faster when believers came under intense persecution.

> …On that day a great persecution broke out against the church in Jerusalem, and all except the apostles were scattered throughout Judea and Samaria. Acts 8:1.

> Peter, an apostle of Jesus Christ, To God's elect, exiles scattered throughout the provinces of Pontus, Galatia, Cappadocia, Asia and Bithynia, 1 Peter 1:1.

The effect of persecution upon the early church was to scatter the body of believers across diverse territories. The believers spread the Word of God as they moved from place to place.

Many well-meaning respectable Moslems have openly denied there being an Islamic agenda to wipe out all non-Islamic religions. The activities of Boko Haram in West Africa and ISIS in Iraq and Syria have raised more questions than there are answers. However, it is important to note that since the 9/11 attacks on American soil, there has been a surge in hate crimes directed at the Muslim communities in the United States. Many Muslims living in America have often had to endure a campaign of bigotry and humiliation in the media and on the streets. The Church must make sure that in this season when it faces persecution from all quarters, that it does not replicate same against Muslims. The Christian faith enjoins us to be kind toward widows, orphans, and aliens. Without undermining security protocols, we must present Muslims with kindness, respect, fairness and of course, the light of the gospel. Who knows, the Lord may be using Islam to awaken and sharpen the Church. The tensions among the faiths are probably going to intensify and the Church must do its best not to exacerbate the tension.

Besides Islam, in the years to come, the Church will also have to contend with changing societal attitudes. In western civilization, there is a growing apathy towards Christianity and an increasing curiosity toward occultic deities and works. Entertainment, literature, media, and various levels of government are now more open to demonic culture and unfortunately, more intolerant of the mention of the name of Jesus Christ. The challenge here for the Church is to remain in the world and yet, not be of the world. The world is set to become more vexed by a Church that refuses to accept the popular culture of sin and rebellion towards God.

Same sex marriage. The recognition and subsequent legalization of same sex marriage in mostly western countries has brought a lot of challenges to the Church. With this new phenomenon came the threats of lawsuits against churches that refused to marry same sex couples and churches which refused to ordain lesbians and homosexuals as clergy. The US Supreme Court ruled in 2015 that homosexual marriages are a constitutional right. To compound matters, churches that refuse to perform homosexual weddings face the threat of financial loss as insurance companies may refuse to cover them in the event of a lawsuit.

As society becomes more reprobate and continues to endorse sexual immorality as a legal right, true churches of Christ will find themselves facing stiff opposition from the very society they were called to save. As man continues to spiral into deeper darkness, he abhors the churches that preach Jesus Christ, the light of the world. The spirits of the antichrist are fighting hard to ensnare the true living church of Jesus Christ in a battle with fallen humanity's insatiable and voracious appetite for sexual perversion. The ultimate goal may be to sanction and blacklist churches that refuse to compromise on the word of God. Herein, lies the gateway to the path of crisis and persecution coming to the church in this season. Churches that refuse to embrace this mark of the beast may as well prepare for constant harassments from the authorities, including threats to revoke their nonprofit tax-exempt status and other legal benefits.

In *Bob Jones University v. The United States*, the US Supreme Court held that the IRS was justified in revoking the tax-exempt status of Bob Jones University because the University pursued a policy of prohibiting interracial dating and marriages which amounted to racism. The University's claim that the IRS had infringed upon its religious liberty was rejected by the Supreme Court because this racial discrimination in education was contrary to a fundamental national public policy.

If the above reasoning of the Supreme Court were to be applied to same sex marriage, it is not hard to see what the outcome may be. Churches adhering strictly to Biblical principles pertaining to marriage will face the possibility of lawsuits from advocates of same sex marriage claiming discrimination based on their sexual orientation.

Churches must begin to take legal steps to protect themselves from these kinds of lawsuits. This is one crisis that antichrist spirits intend to use to destabilize true Christian churches. The real church can stand on the assurance given by Jesus Christ in Matthew 16:18 that He, Jesus Christ is the One building the church upon the revelation of truth ("this rock") and that the gates of hell shall not prevail against it. Christian leaders must resist the temptation to compromise truth at the expense of being politically correct.

Abortion. Roughly over ten years ago, I had a vision of a large majestic throne with what seemed to be rain falling from the throne. I was unable to see the One that sat on this throne but was moved when I realized that what appeared to be rain were the tears of the One that sat on the throne. Immediately in my spirit, I was told that I must intercede for the land of America because it had shed so much innocent blood. Certainly, it had always been in my consciousness that America had shed so much innocent blood in wars across the globe in its quest to maintain global dominance. I was taken aback because I later perceived that this was God crying with His tears like rain. And the Lord said that the innocent blood America had shed in abortions was more than that it had shed in military campaigns. God was not impressed that the American authorities (and of course, by implication, all other authorities, and governments) had dehumanized the unborn child and disregarded the sanctity of human life, including fetal life. Since the Roe v. Wade US Supreme Court decision legalizing abortion in 1973, America has killed roughly 60 million unborn children.

The US Government has consistently provided federal funding in the form of subsidies to top abortion promoters and providers like the Planned Parenthood Federation. Organizations like Planned Parenthood have pursued a rather aggressive abortion agenda and also, made profits from the sale of discarded fetal parts. A steady stream of abortion income and federal subsidies had ensured that Planned Parenthood's annual revenues exceed over

$1b. Killing unborn babies for money has now become a business.

It got so bad to the point where, thank God, there was an intervention to ban partial birth abortions. Partial birth abortion involves an abortion in the late second trimester or third trimester of pregnancy in which the baby is partially delivered alive. While the baby is partly outside and partly in the mother, the skull is broken, and the brain destroyed. America passed the Partial Birth Abortion Act in 2003 and the US Supreme Court upheld it in 2007. Furthermore, in some states in the US, parental consent is not even required for a minor girl to undergo an abortion procedure.

Just like the blood of Abel crying out to God against Cain that murdered him, is the blood of over 60 million unborn children in America that were never given a chance to fulfill their purpose on earth.

Countries like China, Russia and Vietnam have much higher abortion numbers that the United States. The problem here is that because America, more than any other country, presents an image to the world of being a custodian of morality and righteousness, the rest of the world sees right through its hypocrisy. The US with a somewhat Christian foundation ought to know better. The vision I saw with tears flowing from God's throne shows the heart of God regarding this utter disregard to life at conception. God is grieved.

Traditionally speaking, most churches and church denominations have consistently opposed the policy and practice of widespread abortions. Abortion is a national crisis with grave spiritual implications. The God of the Bible does not approve of it under any guise. Righteousness exalts a nation, but sin is a disgrace to any people (Proverbs 14:34). How is the church to respond to this crisis?

The danger with abortion is that even though most humans may not see it as a problem, God does. God's thoughts and ways are so different from ours and God will not lower His standards and give man a pat on the back for violating His will. God's grievance in this area is rising and believers in Christ must intercede for the land not to be consumed by His wrath. So-called Christians and church goers report the highest rates of abortions. In terms of percentages, abortions are higher among Christian women than among women of other faiths or no religious persuasion of any sort. God is coming to visit His church in this hour and it will not be a pleasant visit. The church that has distorted the voice of God and called good evil and evil good, is due for a massive shaking from its very foundations. In this hour, God is set to purge His church with fire that it may come forth as pure gold. God uses persecution that the enemy meant for evil, to sharpen the saints.

Personal Crises

The wave of crises coming to nations will no doubt, have far reaching political, social, and economic consequences.

Individuals will feel the weight of their nation's burdens. Many will swim in one crisis after another and not see a way out. This is the time to get closer to God more than ever before. Believers in Christ will see their faith tested and stretched beyond endurance. To survive this crisis, we must be strong in the Lord and in the power of His might (Ephesians 6:10).

In his second letter to the church in Corinth, the Apostle Paul wrote thus:

We do not want you to be uninformed, brothers, about the hardships we suffered in the province of Asia. We were under great pressure, far beyond our ability to endure, so that we despaired even of life. Indeed, in our hearts we felt the sentence of death. But this happened that we might not rely on ourselves but on God, who raises the dead. He has delivered us from such a deadly peril, and He will deliver us. O Him, we have set our hope that He will continue to deliver us. 2 Corinthians 1:8-10.

[8] We are hard pressed on every side, but not crushed; perplexed, but not in despair; [9] persecuted, but not abandoned; struck down, but not destroyed. [10] We always carry around in our body the death of Jesus, so that the life of Jesus may also be revealed in our body. [11] For we who are alive are always being given over to death for Jesus' sake, so that his life may also be revealed in our mortal body. 2 Corinthians 4:8-10.

The Apostle Paul wrote about afflictions and persecution he had to endure even to the very point of death. Paul's faith rested in God's word and he knew by faith that God is a God that watches over His word to perform it. Crisis will test your level of faith. We are in the last days (the beginning of birth pains phase: Matthew 24:8) and these are perilous times. The Holy Spirit has given ample time and warning of the danger that is ahead. Crisis may not necessarily warn you that it is coming. However, if you have been carefully following world events including increase in terrorism, global economic crises, environmental degradation, and political unrests to name but a few, you have a fair warning that all is not well. You need sufficient time to prepare for crisis. God in His mercy as omniscient God has chosen to warn His people to be prepared.

It is very easy to get into crisis but quite difficult to come out of it. In the 1960s, American society began to adopt a liberal approach toward hard drugs and more people began to experiment with the use of substances like heroin, cocaine, and marijuana. This started as a crisis and later graduated to a war on drugs. The war on drugs metamorphosed into a multibillion dollar business with the respective stakeholders unwilling to see the end of the war. Huge profits are being made on both sides of the war and hence, what started as a crisis has now become what is called, a lingering crisis. Do not be surprised that there are others that profit from your crisis.

We are not to fear the coming of any crisis. God uses crisis to strengthen us and make us wiser. As a skilled potter molds the clay, God uses crisis to mold us into the image of Christ that we may be Christlike. Crisis thus, will force you to change the way you think and value things. Crisis is a character builder. It will make you shed off habits and toxic relationships that are ungodly. Crisis makes you discover who you are and what you are capable of. A crisis will show you who is for you and who is not for you. Prior to crisis, everyone appears to be your friend. When crisis comes, the fair-weather friends quickly disappear.

Here are a few tips to remember in a personal crisis:

1. Tribulations of the righteous are for a moment (2 Corinthians 4:17-18).

2. Crisis will require faith (Hebrews 11:6).

3. Crisis will require patience and you must avoid complaining or murmuring (1 Corinthians 10:10).

4. You must not compromise or shrink back (Hebrews 10:35-39).

5. During crisis, you must still develop yourself spiritually. Polish your spiritual gifts and still allow God to use you.

6. Remain in Christ.

7. The crisis is designed for your personal development and to usher you into abundant life.

Prayer Points to Tackle and Avert Upcoming Crises

1. Heavenly Father, position me, my family, my church, and my business at the right place at the right time in the name of Jesus.

2. Heavenly Father, I intercede for my nation and ask for Your great mercy to send revival into my nation in the name of Jesus Christ.

3. Lord Jesus, You said that in this world, I will have trouble but in You, I will have peace. Lord Jesus fill me with Your peace that surpasses all understanding so that I will not panic when times of testing come my way.

4. In the name of Jesus Christ, I shall be in the ark whenever the judgment of God visits this perverse generation.

5. As I dwell in the secret place of the Most High, Holy Spirit in the name of Jesus, shield me and those that trust in the Lord from all terrorist attacks.

6. Heavenly Father, expose and frustrate all plans of the enemy to launch terrorist attacks against the Church of the Living God in the mighty name of Jesus Christ.

7. Heavenly Father, I pray that God-fearing leaders be elected into office in my nation and that abominations like same sex marriage and abortions that the laws uphold will be reversed in the mighty name of Jesus Christ.

8. Heavenly Father, just as you prepared Joseph for the crisis of famine that was to come upon Egypt and gave him wisdom, prepare me for any crisis that I am destined to go through and give me wisdom to overcome the crisis in Jesus name.

9. In the name of Jesus, I reject the enemy's agenda of affliction and cover myself with the blood of Jesus.

10. In the name of Jesus, I put on the whole armor of God and with the shield of faith, quench every fiery dart that the wicked shoots at me to cause crisis in my life.

11. Holy Spirit, make me invisible before my enemies in the name of Jesus.

12. Heavenly Father, give me the wisdom and the courage to profit from crises that will visit the world in the name of Jesus.

13. When men shall say that there is a casting down, I shall say that there is a lifting up and I shall experience promotion in Jesus' name.

14. I shall not die, but live, and declare the works of the Lord in the mighty name of Jesus Christ.

15. In the mighty name of Jesus Christ, let every evil work of the Illuminati and all other occult groups working hard to create global crisis be frustrated and brought to nothing.

16. Jehovah Jireh, let there be a supernatural increase for the Church and the people of God in the time of financial crisis, in the name of Jesus Christ.

17. Lord Jesus Christ, equip and finance Your Church that the gospel may advance regardless of tribulation.

18. Our Father which art in Heaven, lead me not into temptation but deliver me from evil in the name of Jesus.

CHAPTER TWO

You Cannot Afford to Be Ignorant

The price to pay for being ignorant is often quite excessive. Ignorance is not bliss. Ignorance, often, plays a key role in determining levels and degrees of bondage. If you do not know that you are in a crisis, the crisis is likely to persist and escalate. Others may warn you of the danger that you may be in, but if you choose to remain ignorant or adamant, chances are that you will not appreciate the need to exercise caution or to seek for solution. In crisis, you must aspire for both intellectual and spiritual awareness of the nature and characteristics of the crisis. Also, seek for an understanding of who the stakeholders in your crisis are and what their interests are. You will need wisdom and understanding to navigate through the daunting dark tunnels of a crisis.

The discerning heart seeks knowledge, but the mouth of a fool feeds on folly. Proverbs 15:14.

Do not forsake wisdom, and she will protect you; love her, and she will watch over you. Wisdom is supreme; therefore get wisdom. Though it cost all you have, get understanding. Proverbs 4:6-7.

Until you begin to seek knowledge and understanding of root causes rather than just viewing things on the surface, you run the risk of being subject to deception by all that is going on around you. There is a strong connection between ignorance, deception, and bondage. Ignorance feeds crisis. To make an exodus from a crisis, you will require wisdom, knowledge and understanding. These three things will teach you where to go to for godly counsel, how to pray and what approach to follow. Being wise in your own eyes is a flaw that often prolongs crisis.

My people are destroyed for lack of knowledge: because thou hast rejected knowledge, I will also reject thee, that thou shalt be no priest to me: seeing thou hast forgotten the law of thy God, I will also forget thy children: Hosea 4:6.

Many lives have been destroyed for lack of knowledge. When a person rejects knowledge, it is often because of not having a teachable spirit. The person wants to continue doing things the same way and yet expects a different result. In these perilous times, crises are multiplying on all levels, and you cannot afford to be ignorant. Without knowledge, wisdom cannot be applied. Wisdom is the application of knowledge. Many are in ignorance because they have not sought knowledge. Knowledge inspires understanding. Wisdom then applies knowledge and understanding to get you out of life's crises and to keep you somewhat insulated from life's crises.

Ignorance Could Be Very Costly

When you are ignorant of a situation presenting itself, you will see the bait and not see the trap. The bait is appealing. If all you see and are cognizant of is the bait, then you are liable to be caught in the trap. For a trap to be effective, it must present a rather appealing bait while concealing its peril. Many have found themselves in crisis because of the bait that they swallowed. This bait could be temptation, deception, offense, rebellion, unforgiveness and other things that may seem so justifiable and yet, carry with them, poison.

In Acts 27, Paul, and other prisoners in the company of sailors and soldiers set for Rome by ship. Paul warned about the danger of continuing this sea voyage, considering the inclement weather, but his warnings were ignored. Paul's warnings were not taken seriously perhaps because, he was not known as an expert sailor or a sailor for that matter.

In Acts 27:13-14, it is recorded that 'when the south wind blew softly, supposing that they had obtained their purpose, loosing thence, they sailed close by Crete. But not long after there arose against it a tempestuous wind, called Euroclydon.'

Here, the south wind that blew softly was the bait. It encouraged them to set sail and thus, enter a severe crisis. What they did not anticipate or bargain for came upon them with such suddenness and force. The Euroclydon was the trap that resulted in a severe crisis at sea. The pleasant wind that blew softly ushered in a hurricane. Paul knew what the experts did not know. In Acts 27:10, Paul told the sailors that the voyage will be with hurt and much damage to the ship, property, and lives. If they had listened to Paul who had the knowledge, they would have avoided the Euroclydon crisis. How did Paul get this knowledge? Paul received this knowledge through his close fellowship with God (Acts 27:23). In Acts 27, a lot was lost because the right knowledge was not applied from the start. The way you respond to the bait often determines how you relate to crisis. Some seek to swallow the bait without being ensnared. Many mice have eaten the cheese without being caught by the trap. However, continuous engaging in risky behavior will invariably lead to dire consequences.

In May 1960, Chile suffered two major earthquakes with a magnitude of 9.5 on the Richter scale. The earthquakes took place deep at sea and had initially caused the Pacific Ocean to recede from the shore rather quickly. This withdrawal of the Pacific Ocean from the shore caused a lot of fish and aquatic life to be stranded on the seabed. As a result, many excited Chilean villagers, including children, rushed to gather fish in their baskets. During their excitement of gathering free fish, a second earthquake struck, and it was too late for many to escape. Water, 60 feet high and traveling at roughly 200 miles per hour overtook many and destroyed the village.

The Chilean villagers did not anticipate this calamity. The returning waters were much taller and faster than them. This crisis was a catastrophe that brought other crises with it: crisis of living amid devastation and recovery efforts. There are crises that have come upon people suddenly and that have brought a series of other crises in their path. Crises tend to be connected to one another and one must understand the connections that feed a crisis. If the Chilean villagers understood the possibility of an aftershock, they probably would have prepared for it rather than gather fish in the very path of the tsunami that was in the making.

Crisis often comes without warning and so there is the need to be prepared always. There are times however, when crisis warns that it is coming. In the book of Genesis, Joseph had advised Pharaoh that Egypt was about to enjoy seven years of abundance followed by seven years of severe famine. Pharaoh was fortunate enough to have had seven years of abundance to prepare for the expected seven years of crisis. In addition, and even more importantly, he was fortunate to have had the right knowledge of what was to come. Otherwise, the seven years of abundance may have been squandered with the expectation that there will always be an abundance in the land. With this knowledge and the right application of this knowledge, the crisis that Egypt faced was of a lesser severity. The interesting thing about the seven-year famine crisis in Egypt is that while it impoverished the people, it enriched

Joseph. (Genesis 47:13-26). Joseph profited from the very crisis that reduced others to nothing. This was simply because Joseph knew something by revelation that others did not.

Means of Knowledge

Knowledge can be acquired through study, experience, education, and revelation. God forbids the acquiring of knowledge through occultic and demonic channels.

Study. In these times of uncertainties, it is very important that we study not only the word of God but also our environment, the signs of the times, institutions, political, economic, and financial systems, global shifts, and people of influence. As we study these things that influence life on planet earth, we must also ask God for revelation knowledge coupled with understanding.

But mark this: There will be terrible times in the last days. 2 Timothy 3:1.

The Bible makes us understand that there will be terrible times in the last days. If you agree with me that these are the last days, then you must plan for terrible times. By a simple study of the Scriptures, we get the knowledge that the days ahead of us shall witness terrible and perilous times, wars and rumors of wars, famines, earthquakes, other natural disasters, and an increase in the activities of false prophets and false teachers. To be forewarned is to be forearmed and so with this knowledge, God puts us in a vantage position to prepare for crises. We must not be taken by surprise. We must operate from a platform of knowledge to minimize confusion and deception in the wake of a crisis. We need quantitative as well as qualitative knowledge in navigating through a crisis and planning an exodus therefrom.

Today, many nations are in various crises because their policies were not founded on accurate information but were based on assumptions. With the passage of time, those assumptions proved false or unsustainable. For instance, many third world countries were encouraged by developed countries to embark on white elephant projects that had to be financed by loans with outrageous repayment terms. Many of these third world countries swallowed the bait, assumed that surrounding conditions will remain the same or improve, only to discover a fast-changing world making unexpected and increasing demands upon their fragile economies. Many third world country policy makers and high-ranking government officials worked hand in hand with first world banking institutions and multinational corporations to facilitate capital flight out of the third world. Lack of knowledge, corruption and backroom conspiracies have placed many third world economies in severe crises. Those that had knowledge and that were willing to advise these countries were often shunned away or relegated to irrelevant positions. In the multitude of counselors is safety (Proverbs 11:14). These countries chose to transact business outside of the safety net by their ignoring the multitude of godly counselors.

Just like an individual, when a nation faces a crisis, it needs to understand the underlying currents feeding the crisis. To understand a matter, often requires one diligently searching out the matter and gaining a knowledge of the matter. To understand a matter, the root causes, other causes, the stakeholders and their interests, its scope, its objective and other pertinent factors will have to be examined with a degree of scrutiny.

In 1 Chronicles 12, fighters from the various tribes of Israel came together to support David as king instead of Saul. The various tribes, except for the tribe of Issachar, came with thousands of armed men to support David. In 1 Chronicles 12:32 it is recorded that the tribe of Issachar came with 200 chiefs and their relatives. Issachar came with the least number of soldiers to assist David become king. In 1 Chronicles 12:32, it says that the men of Issachar understood the times and knew what Israel should do. They understood, and they knew. When you understand something, you will know it better. Their understanding and knowledge probably put them at a position where they knew that it was not the strength of numbers that will give David the throne. When you understand and know a matter, less of heavy lifting may be required. The men of Issachar knew. People that know, do not have to guess. They do not have to assume. They know.

You are bigger than your crisis. Greater is He that is in you than he that is in the world (1 John 4:4) and Christ has gone ahead of you to overcome trials, tribulations, and crises of this world (John 16:33). During crisis, do not curse and despise your crisis. Rather, be a good student, study it and learn and profit from it. Understand the source of your crisis and begin to diminish and destroy those things that feed crisis in your life. Do not leave things to chance and expect a crisis to just go away. That is mere wishful thinking. Take time away from lamenting and as you pray for victory, take time to know, understand and discern all that is going on around you.

Experience. Generally, children have less experience than adults and so are more susceptible to and vulnerable in crisis. Their vulnerability is heightened in the absence of any form of guidance. There are certain matters that are known by mere repetition. Many may not have had the opportunity to go through the process of repetition in question. Experience, it is often said, is a good teacher. When a toddler touches live electricity or fire, he needs no one to remind him not to repeat his desire to experiment with electricity or fire. Experience reminds him and has taught him that good lesson he will never forget. Therefore, it is of importance to find people that have gone through a similar scenario so that you can learn from them. When you study the reactions of others that have been in crisis before you, you are learning from their experience. The Bible is filled with characters such as political leaders, prophets, believers, and ordinary people that went through one form of crisis or the other. Some of the crises were self-inflicted, some were because of factors beyond their control. Nonetheless, by revisiting their experience, you will appreciate what works with God and what does not.

Experience is the teacher that says that if you keep doing the same thing, you will keep getting the same result. When you have learned from experience, you will know to change unprofitable ways to attract profitable outcomes.

Education. This is more than mere passing through an institution of learning. In fact, many of our institution of learning have not trained their enrollees to be true scholars. So-called historical facts have not been examined and questioned thoroughly. Many schools offer a curriculum which at best, may pass for indoctrination rather than an education. Many of our schools have not equipped their enrollees to face the challenges of everyday living in pluralistic societies. Students graduate with degrees in Finance and Economics and do not have the slightest clue of how to behave in a financial crisis. With the kinds of crises that are on the horizon, a mere formal school education will not suffice to enable you overcome impending crises. You are going to have to learn to be an independent student. You are going to have to learn to engage in critical thinking and to commit your ways to God. The understanding provided by a formal education, as great as it is, is limited.

Trust in the Lord with all your heart and lean not on your own understanding; in all your ways acknowledge him, and he will make your paths straight. Proverbs 3:5-6.

This is what the Lord says: "Cursed is the one who trusts in man, who depends on flesh for his strength and whose heart turns away from the Lord. Jeremiah 17:5.

In your crisis, you cannot put your trust in man and in your own understanding. You cannot put your confidence in your connections, your social status, your education, or your material resources. God remains the only One that can direct a man out of Egypt into Canaan.

Revelation. God can reveal matters of the past, present, and future to whosoever He chooses to. God's revelation is not limited to Christians. Christians will be shortchanging themselves if they think that God cannot use unbelievers to reveal truth. In the Old Testament, God gave revelation to pagan kings such as Pharaoh and Nebuchadnezzar. They had the revelation, but they did not have the understanding regarding what it meant.

> [15] Pharaoh said to Joseph, "I had a dream, and no one can interpret it. But I have heard it said of you that when you hear a dream you can interpret it."

> [16] "I cannot do it," Joseph replied to Pharaoh, "but God will give Pharaoh the answer he desires."

> [17] Then Pharaoh said to Joseph, "In my dream I was standing on the bank of the Nile, [18] when out of the river there came up seven cows, fat and sleek, and

they grazed among the reeds. ¹⁹ After them, seven other cows came up—scrawny and very ugly and lean. I had never seen such ugly cows in all the land of Egypt. ²⁰ The lean, ugly cows ate up the seven fat cows that came up first. ²¹ But even after they ate them, no one could tell that they had done so; they looked just as ugly as before. Then I woke up.

²² "In my dream I saw seven heads of grain, full and good, growing on a single stalk. ²³ After them, seven other heads sprouted—withered and thin and scorched by the east wind. ²⁴ The thin heads of grain swallowed up the seven good heads. I told this to the magicians, but none of them could explain it to me."

²⁵ Then Joseph said to Pharaoh, "The dreams of Pharaoh are one and the same. God has revealed to Pharaoh what he is about to do. ²⁶ The seven good cows are seven years, and the seven good heads of grain are seven years; it is one and the same dream. ²⁷ The seven lean, ugly cows that came up afterward are seven years, and so are the seven worthless heads of grain scorched by the east wind: They are seven years of famine.

²⁸ "It is just as I said to Pharaoh: God has shown Pharaoh what he is about to do. ²⁹ Seven years of great abundance are coming throughout the land of Egypt, ³⁰ but seven years of famine will follow them. Then all the abundance in Egypt will be forgotten,

and the famine will ravage the land. [31] The abundance in the land will not be remembered, because the famine that follows it will be so severe. [32] The reason the dream was given to Pharaoh in two forms is that the matter has been firmly decided by God, and God will do it soon.

[33] "And now let Pharaoh look for a discerning and wise man and put him in charge of the land of Egypt. [34] Let Pharaoh appoint commissioners over the land to take a fifth of the harvest of Egypt during the seven years of abundance. [35] They should collect all the food of these good years that are coming and store up the grain under the authority of Pharaoh, to be kept in the cities for food. [36] This food should be held in reserve for the country, to be used during the seven years of famine that will come upon Egypt, so that the country may not be ruined by the famine."

[37] The plan seemed good to Pharaoh and to all his officials. [38] So Pharaoh asked them, "Can we find anyone like this man, one in whom is the spirit of God[a]?"

[39] Then Pharaoh said to Joseph, "Since God has made all this known to you, there is no one so discerning and wise as you. [40] You shall be in charge of my palace, and all my people are to submit to your orders. Only with respect to the throne will I be greater than you." Genesis 41: 15-39

It took the Spirit of God working through Joseph to interpret what the revelations Pharaoh received in a dream truly meant. Pharaoh received information from God through a dream. He had knowledge but lacked the understanding. He had bits and pieces of information but lacked the ability to make sense out of it all. The grace of God upon the life of Joseph provided understanding to Pharaoh through the dream's interpretation.

In the case of King Nebuchadnezzar's dream, it was quite different. Perhaps, the king had forgotten the dream and needed a reminder. However, the king refused to tell the content of his dream to the wise men of Babylon. The wise men of Babylon were stuck because without knowledge of the king's dream, understanding of what the dream meant could not be provided. This was a crisis especially as King Nebuchadnezzar was threatening to execute all the wise men of Babylon for not having knowledge of his dream, and thus, not providing the understanding of what the dream meant. In a crisis, you must first know the pertinent facts and the facts that are in issue before you start to understand what is going on.

First is to have knowledge and then, understanding followed by wisdom. In the case of Pharaoh's dream, knowledge was received by Pharaoh sharing with Joseph what he dreamt. The understanding of the dream came by Joseph's interpretation. Now that there was knowledge and understanding, the atmosphere was conducive for wisdom to be applied. Joseph was now able to apply wisdom and he did so by suggesting that Pharaoh appoint a wise and discerning man to oversee the land of Egypt. This gave Egypt the ability to survive this severe famine. Now with King Nebuchadnezzar, the story was different. Without any knowledge of the dream, there could be no understanding; let alone, application of wisdom. In Daniel 2, Daniel went before God to ask for help in this matter. God gave Daniel the knowledge, the understanding, and the wisdom regarding Nebuchadnezzar's dream. God provided Daniel with knowledge, understanding and wisdom all at once by revelation.

[26] The king asked Daniel (also called Belteshazzar), "Are you able to tell me what I saw in my dream and interpret it?"

[27] Daniel replied, "No wise man, enchanter, magician or diviner can explain to the king the mystery he has asked about, [28] but there is a God in heaven who reveals mysteries. He has shown King Nebuchadnezzar what will happen in days to come. Your dream and the visions that passed through your mind as you were lying in bed are these:

[29] "As Your Majesty was lying there, your mind turned to things to come, and the revealer of mysteries showed you what is going to happen. [30] As for me, this mystery has been revealed to me, not because I have greater wisdom than anyone else alive, but so that Your Majesty may know the

interpretation and that you may understand what went through your mind.

[31] "Your Majesty looked, and there before you stood a large statue—an enormous, dazzling statue, awesome in appearance. [32] The head of the statue was made of pure gold, its chest and arms of silver, its belly and thighs of bronze, [33] its legs of iron, its feet partly of iron and partly of baked clay. [34] While you were watching, a rock was cut out, but not by human hands. It struck the statue on its feet of iron and clay and smashed them. [35] Then the iron, the clay, the bronze, the silver and the gold were all broken to pieces and became like chaff on a threshing floor in the summer. The wind swept them away without leaving a trace. But the rock that struck the statue became a huge mountain and filled the whole earth. [36] "This was the dream, and now we will interpret it to the king. [37] Your Majesty, you are the king of kings. The God of heaven has given you dominion and power and might and glory; [38] in your hands he has placed all mankind and the beasts of the field and the birds in the sky. Wherever they live, he has made you ruler over them all. You are that head of gold.

[39] "After you, another kingdom will arise, inferior to yours. Next, a third kingdom, one of bronze, will rule over the whole earth. [40] Finally, there will be a fourth kingdom, strong as iron—for iron breaks and smashes everything—and as iron breaks things

to pieces, so it will crush and break all the others. [41] Just as you saw that the feet and toes were partly of baked clay and partly of iron, so this will be a divided kingdom; yet it will have some of the strength of iron in it, even as you saw iron mixed with clay. [42] As the toes were partly iron and partly clay, so this kingdom will be partly strong and partly brittle. [43] And just as you saw the iron mixed with baked clay, so the people will be a mixture and will not remain united, any more than iron mixes with clay.

[44] "In the time of those kings, the God of heaven will set up a kingdom that will never be destroyed, nor will it be left to another people. It will crush all those kingdoms and bring them to an end, but it will itself endure forever. [45] This is the meaning of the vision of the rock cut out of a mountain, but not by human hands—a rock that broke the iron, the bronze, the clay, the silver and the gold to pieces.

"The great God has shown the king what will take place in the future. The dream is true and its interpretation is trustworthy." Daniel 2: 26-45.

The crises on the way to visit mankind shortly will require you to operate in the spiritual realm where you can receive revelation from God. How was Daniel able to receive so much from God? To answer this question, we must look at the lifestyle of Daniel. Daniel was a humble man. He was a man that diligently sought God in fasting and prayer. Daniel was a man that refused to compromise with the evil suggestions and culture of his time. God is pleased to reveal deep mysteries to men of such character.

The wave of crises that is coming will hit humanity on a personal, community, national and global level. You must be prepared. Crisis on a personal level can be averted and minimized. However, there is a global crisis that is at our doorsteps and we will need divine knowledge, understanding and wisdom to go through the crisis. One crisis that is coming to humanity with such incredible speed is God's judgment. Wealth and status cannot insulate anyone from God's judgment. As the currents of divine judgments begin to visit the earth, it is not so much what you know and understand that will matter. It is not what Daniel knew that mattered. It was who he knew. In the times of crises, you must know God. It is God that will put a hedge of protection around you to shield you from the fiery darts of crisis.

Many Christians have been misled into thinking that Christianity is centered on prosperity and earthly riches. Jesus Christ made it clear in the Scriptures that a man's life does not consist in the abundance of his possessions. Many Christians ignorantly believe that not having certain earthly possessions means that they are not enjoying the abundant life that Christ had promised in John 10:10. This ignorance and lack of understanding produces a frustration, fueled by a lack of contentment, that they are missing something in life. Colossians 3:2 admonishes us to set our minds on things above and not on earthly things. When a mind is constantly set on earthly things, that mind will see crisis even when heaven says there is no crisis. Many that have created their own crisis in their minds, in their thinking and in their imaginations, will do well to be transformed by the renewing of their minds into the mind of Christ.

Truth be told, when Christ calls a man, He bids him to come and die! When you are living as a child of light in a world of darkness, you are living through daily crisis. Deciding to live for Christ in today's world will cost you much.

> Then He said to them all: "If anyone would come after Me, he must deny himself and take up his cross daily and follow Me. For whoever wants to save his life will lose it, but whoever loses his life for Me will save it." Luke 9:23-24.

Christ made it clear that He came that you might have life and have life more abundantly. This promise of abundant life requires that you go through the personal crisis of daily surrendering your will to that of Christ. It is this Christ induced crisis, triggered by your obedience, that enables you rise above worldly crisis.

Prayers for Spiritual Revelation and Discernment

1. In the name of Jesus Christ, I ask for a spirit of discernment to know the true from the false.

2. Holy Spirit, in the name of Jesus Christ, open my spiritual eyes to see those who are for me and those who are against me.

3. Heavenly Father, as I call upon You in the name of Jesus and in the day of trouble, open my eyes to see great and mighty things that I know not.

4. Lord Jesus, speak to me in dreams and visions and give me the understanding of dreams and visions.

5. Heavenly Father, give me a spirit of wisdom and revelation and enlighten the eyes of my heart that I may know my life purpose in the mighty name of Jesus Christ.

6. In the name of Jesus Christ, I forbid the spirits of stupor, confusion, and legalism from blocking my spiritual vision and claim freedom from all such spirits by the power in the blood of Jesus.

7. O Lord, in the name of Jesus, show me Your glory.

8. Holy Spirit fill me with the knowledge and understanding of the Word of God that I may not be deceived by ignorance in Jesus name.

9. Holy Spirit, give me discernment to test the spirits in the name of Jesus Christ, that I may not be deceived by a false prophet.

10. Holy Spirit, in the name of Jesus Christ, expose every deception and darkness within and around me.

11. In the name of Jesus, I forgive all that have offended me for I am not ignorant of the devil's devices to keep me in bondage.

12. Heavenly Father, I desire the spiritual gifts that I may prophesy in the name of Jesus.

13. Holy Spirit, take me deeper in the things of God I pray in Jesus name.

14. O Lord, reveal unto me the plan of the enemy in their secret places, I ask in the name of Jesus.

15. Holy Spirit, help me to always be ahead of my enemies in the name of Jesus.

16. The light shineth in the darkness and the darkness comprehendeth it not. Every darkness blocking my way be destroyed now by the light of God in the name of Jesus.

17. Heavenly Father, let Your Word be a lamp unto my feet and a light unto my path in the name of Jesus.

18. Holy Spirit, in Jesus' name, expose Satan and his agents when they appear before me as angels of light and ministers of righteousness.

19. Heavenly Father, You are the revealer of mysteries, as I walk with You faithfully, reveal Your mysteries and secrets to me in the name of Jesus.

20. Heavenly Father, give me understanding that I may never fall into the snare of the fowler in Jesus' name.

CHAPTER THREE

Coming Out of Oppression

¹⁸ Then I looked up, and there before me were four horns. ¹⁹ I asked the angel who was speaking me, "What are these?"

He answered me, "These are the horns that scattered Judah, Israel and Jerusalem."

²⁰ Then the Lord showed me four craftsmen. ²¹ I asked, "What are these coming to do?"

He answered, "These are the horns that scattered Judah so that no one could raise their head, but the craftsmen have come to terrify them and throw down these horns of the nations who lifted up their horns against the land of Judah to scatter its people." Zechariah 1:18-21.

The Prophet Zechariah looked up and saw four horns. You need to look up to see things that are beyond you. Now that Zechariah had seen four horns, he needed understanding and sought to know the meaning of the four horns. The source of Zechariah's understanding was from the Lord. The angel of the Lord revealed to Zechariah that these four horns represented Gentile nations that opposed Judah, Israel, and Jerusalem. Horns are symbols of power. God allowed them to chastise God's people. These four horns represented four Gentile powers during Israel's history, namely: Egypt, Assyria, Medo-Persia, and Babylon. Rome was to come subsequently. These Gentile powers oppressed Israel for various reasons and it took divine providence for Israel to exit out of their oppression. Zechariah was shown four craftsmen (carpenters) that had come to terrify and destroy these oppressor-nations.

Egypt

In the book of Genesis, we see how Joseph was sold by his own household into bondage in the land of Egypt. While in prison on trumped up charges, his spiritual gifts were brought to Pharaoh, the king of Egypt's attention. Proverbs 18:16 says that a man's gifts make room for him and brings him before great men. This was the case with Joseph. When faced with a crisis, you must use that which God has given you (the anointing, spiritual gifts, abilities, and skills) to make room for you and bring you before decision makers. Pharaoh was very pleased with Joseph and gladly welcomed Joseph's entire family into the fertile lands of Egypt.

Egypt initially welcomed the people of God and then, enslaved them. The Israelites went to Egypt because they were looking for a means of sustenance to alleviate their lack. Egypt offered the Israelites false promises and a false sense of security and eventually subjected them to a slavery of over 400 years. By the time appointed for Israel's exodus from Egypt, Egyptian culture had become so ingrained in the minds of Israel. Even though Israel left Egypt, they still carried Egypt inside of them. When Moses went up to the mountain to meet with God and receive the Ten Commandments, the people of Israel built a golden calf as an idol to worship. Israel had left Egypt, but her heart was still with the gods of Egypt.

While transitioning from Egypt to Canaan, the children of Israel were fond of looking back in the direction of Egypt. It is amazing how a problem that we have been immersed in for a considerable period can become like a second nature to us. The problem, as chronic as it may be, can become a comfort zone to guard against the unfamiliar. Often, solutions dwell in the realm of the unfamiliar. So here was Israel, often complaining that they preferred to return to Egypt. The promise of a solution in Canaan seemed almost unattainable to them because they failed to operate in faith. Now faith is being sure of what we hope for and certain of what we do not see (Hebrews 11:1). To come out of a crisis, you must have faith. A solution you do not believe in will not work for you. The Israelites, during their affliction, desired to settle for less. They were filled with unbelief and subsequently with fear to the extent that they were unwilling to possess their inheritance. Unbelief often, gives birth to fear and fear gives birth to an unwillingness to fight for the best.

To come out of Egypt, God has raised a craftsman, a carpenter, a man, a pastor, a prophet, a Moses, an angel to assist you. You must not undermine the craftsman that God has raised up for you. Zechariah looked up and saw four craftsmen. When you look up, who do you see? Do you see more horns, or do you see some craftsmen coming with help? You must know who your craftsman-carpenter is. In crisis, do not let the devil impose the wrong craftsman upon you. The wrong craftsman works secretly in collaboration with the horns that are against you. The wrong craftsmen are the false apostles, deceitful workmen, masquerading as apostles of Christ (2 Corinthians 11:13).

Egypt is about the worst form of captivity. It offers promises that are never fulfilled. In Exodus, we see how Pharaoh made several promises to let the children of Israel go and how he kept breaking his very own promises. Any time a promise is made, hope arises. Any time a promise is broken, hope is crushed. Hope deferred makes the heart sick (Proverbs 13:12). Christ is the true Hope and real security. At the Passover, Pharaoh could no longer renege on his promise to let the children of Israel go. It was at Passover when the choice blood (first born son) of the oppressor was spilt that the oppressor released the oppressed from oppression. Christ is our Passover Lamb (1 Corinthians 5:7).

The Israelites set out from Rameses on the fifteenth day of the first month, the day after Passover. They marched out boldly in full view of all the Egyptians, who were burying all their firstborn, whom the Lord had struck down among them; for the Lord had brought judgment on their gods. Numbers 33:3-4.

In coming out of crisis induced by the Egyptian strongman called Bondage, you must cry out to God to execute judgment on their gods. Their gods are often Wealth, Fame, and Status. When the oppressor is disconnected from the source of his power in the spirit realm, the process begins for the liberation of the victims of his oppression.

Medo-Persia

Compared to the other nations that oppressed Israel, Medo-Persia appeared to have some iota of benevolence. It offered a porous freedom to Israel in the sense that it set a date for Israel's freedom to cease by annihilation. The Israelites were free to live as vassal subjects, but a law had been passed that on a certain day, they all were to be exterminated. This is like the turkey that is given rich food by its master not knowing that a day, (in America, typically Thanksgiving Day), has been set aside for its demise. Medo-Persia as seen in the book of Esther, was kind of a slow poison that drained the people of God and created a fear of pursuing freedom and victory until when pushed to the wall. This type of oppression is quite deceptive in the sense that it suggests defeat even when freedom is offered. It creates an environment of fear that discourages pursuing deliverance as reprisals are often threatened.

Esther, in a sense, was the craftsman that God raised to deliver Israel from the hand of Haman, an enemy of the Jews and from King Artaxerxes, a king that really was not passionate about the plight of the Jews. The people of Israel rallied round Esther, through fasting and prayers, as she interceded for Israel before the king. Esther's plea resulted in the Jews being authorized to resist and carry arms to fight against forces of the State on the day designated for their extermination. In your crisis, you must know who your Esther is that is pleading your case before the King. Do not frustrate the appointed person assigned to bring you out of crisis.

Some people have remained in crisis because they refused to recognize their divine helper. If the men of Israel in the time of Queen Esther refused to cooperate with Esther on the basis that she was a woman, Israel may have been exterminated by her enemies.

A good number of men have refused to receive godly ministry from a woman and have remained in their pitiful circumstances. God uses the weak things of this world to confound the strong and the foolish things of this world to confound the wise. God uses the things that are not to confound those things that are so that no man may glory before Him (1 Corinthians 1:27-29). Others have refused godly ministry from another because that other was of a different nationality, social status, education status or other background. In a crisis, often, the solution may lie with someone outside of your comfort zone. You must humble yourself to receive help from whatever instrument God has prepared for your deliverance.

Assyria

The purpose of Assyria was to destroy and put an end to many nations (Isaiah 10:5-7). Assyria represents the crisis of limitation and stagnation (2 Kings 18:31-33). In 2 Kings 18, the King of Assyria sought a false peace with Israel that gave Assyria the right to be Israel's master in exchange for Israel being allowed to eat food that belonged to Israel. Assyria was a threat to Israel's survival and offered Israel a right to exist only if Israel agreed to be subject to Assyrian domination and oppression. Today, many are under this form of oppression. They have lost the joy of following their own divine destiny and have been subject to forces much stronger than they are.

If you struck a deal with the King of Assyria that has now limited you and kept you stagnant, you need one of the four carpenters of Zechariah 1 to set you free. The King of Assyria uses intimidation to make others swear ungodly oaths and enter evil covenants that puts them and their descendants at his mercy for the rest of their lives. The prince of Assyria is that spirit, that principality that discourages believers from fighting. It makes believers want to give up the fight and yet, pretend to be fighting. Assyria promotes through intimidation, a form of godliness that denies the power thereof. Assyria does this by intimidating its victim to think like the world in order not to suffer disadvantages like friends mocking you, relatives abandoning you and the rest of the world thinking you are silly.

To come out of the bondage of Assyria, you must begin to renounce every covenant you or your ancestors made with the prince of Assyria. Just like angelic reinforcement was sent against the prince of Persia in Daniel 10, you must cry out for the Lord to send power to break the oppression of Assyrian bondage.

In referring to the tyranny of Assyria, Isaiah 10:27 says that the yoke shall be destroyed because of the anointing. The anointing is the power of the Holy Spirit. You need the help of the Holy Spirit in moments of crisis. The Holy Spirit is a Teacher, Counselor, and Comforter (John 14:26). The Holy Spirit is the divine helper that empowers you to navigate through a crisis. He will bring a word of knowledge, a word of wisdom, a revelation that will enable you to see the way out of a predicament.

Babylon

Babylon represents idolatry (idol worship, psychic appreciation, witchcraft, and false gods) and confusion (Tower of Babel). Babylon rejects God's word and only accepts it when it is convenient or when there is a benefit in doing so. Babylon led Israel into exile in Babylon and enslaved them in Babylon. Babylon ridiculed Israel in their captivity and urged them to sing the Lord's songs while they were in shackles.

> By the rivers of Babylon we sat and wept when we remembered Zion. There on the poplars we hung our harps, for there our captors asked us for songs, our tormentors demanded songs of joy; they said, "Sing us one of the songs of Zion!" How can we sing the songs of the Lord while in a foreign land? Psalm 137:1-4.

Babylon is the principality that oppresses the saints and still permits them to worship in churches. They worship God but are controlled by Babylon. Despite their serving God, they know that somehow, there is another power that is ordering their steps.

God raised up king Cyrus of Persia to set Israel free from captivity in Babylon. King Cyrus was the craftsman-carpenter that God used to bring Israel out of Babylon. God can use those that do not know Him to deliver you from your predicament. God can even use the wisdom, the finances, the power and other resources of unbelievers to deliver believers from crisis.

In Zechariah 1:20, the Prophet Zechariah was shown four carpenters (craftsmen). For every horn that he was shown, there was a carpenter appointed to subdue that horn. For every enemy of God's people, God has provided a counteracting power adequate to destroy such enemy. The carpenter is the one sent to bring you out of your predicament. The carpenter is that angel, that pastor, that prophet, that mentor, that fellow believer, that unbeliever that God has stirred up to bring you out of the pit. Some have remained in their crisis because they have failed to recognize or appreciate their carpenter. Some have even insulted, fought, and frustrated their carpenters to the point that the carpenters left them where they were, and their conditions grew worse. Be at peace with the one God has sent to help you. Do not frustrate your divine helpers.

The best carpenter is the Word of God. Little wonder, Jesus (the Word) was a carpenter. In any crisis, you must cultivate the habit of looking up to Jesus Christ for direction and assistance. The entrance of God's word into a matter brings light and understanding into that matter (Psalm 119: 130).

Witchcraft Strongholds

Witchcraft essentially is the use of satanic means to control, manipulate and cause evil to others. Witches and wizards have a covenant with Satan to carry out evil assignments and operations. Through magic, divination, and sorcery, they have transferred many people's destinies and imprisoned them in the secret places of darkness. Witchcraft releases demonic spirits to influence our environment and sphere of influence. Witchcraft works to make people think that their crisis is out of the ordinary and that there is no way out.

The queen of witchcraft is Jezebel. Jezebel is a principality that wars against the people of God. In 2 Kings 9, God anointed Jehu as King of Israel to destroy the house of King Ahab and to kill Jezebel. The ministry of Jezebel was to shed the blood of the prophets and other servants of God. In Revelation 2, Christ reprimands the Church in Thyatira for allowing Jezebel, a false prophetess corrupt His servants. The spirit of Jezebel comes with false teachings, deceptive counsel and manipulation to ensure that people remain in bondage.

Crisis induced by witchcraft tends to be recurrent. It will require a high level of spiritual warfare to destroy the strongholds of witchcraft and exit out of the snare. If you are in a battle orchestrated by witchcraft forces, you must begin to fast and pray and walk uprightly before the Lord. You must put on the whole armor of God, walk in the spirit, and begin to wage violent warfare in the spirit against every witchcraft foundation and habitation in your family and in your sphere of influence. You must pray for the power of God to be released to destroy every witchcraft foundation, habitation, stronghold, altar, and device operating to perpetuate crisis in your life.

Curses

Often, when one is experiencing recurring oppression and observes an evil pattern in his life, a curse may be in operation. A curse is an evil pronouncement or ritual that acts as an obstacle to one receiving blessings. An evil spirit is given the assignment of enforcing the curse in the life of the victim. A curse may have its origin in previous generations. Until the curse is challenged, broken, revoked, and destroyed, it will continue to operate against the victim. The effect of many curses is to place their victims in unending crisis or to take them from one crisis after another with little or no breaks. When God allows crisis in our lives, it is not to destroy us but rather, to build us up. On the other hand, satanic crisis is geared toward frustration, a sense of hopelessness, poverty, and destruction.

There is always a reason or cause for a curse.

Like a fluttering sparrow or a darting swallow, an undeserved curse does not come to rest. Proverbs 26:2.

If you are in a crisis that defies all solution, it may be a crisis birthed by a curse. A curse is a terrible thing because it acts as an invisible barrier that hinders one from receiving expected blessings. It will be prudent to search for the root cause of the curse. It may be because of personal sin or the sins of one's ancestors. To break a curse, you must repent of your sins and those of your ancestors and ask God for forgiveness. You must also forgive others that may have sinned against you. In addition, you must renounce all satanic and occultic covenants and objects and pray in faith for the curse to be broken in the name of Jesus Christ.

The Stronghold of Addictions

Addiction is an oppressive stronghold that enforces a dependency upon its victim to engage in destructive patterns of behavior. Addiction comes in the forms of substance abuse, alcohol dependency, gambling, pain killers, gluttony, sex – especially masturbation – and much more. The spirit of addiction works behind the scenes to produce a compulsive desire and craving to engage in destructive addictive habits. People battling addictions see their addiction as a means to escape or cope with the realities of a physical existence. Unfortunately, addiction does not help in overcoming stress and other challenges of life, it only masks them and leads the victim further down the path of degeneration. Circumstances and events can also trigger the need to feed an addiction. An addicted person surrenders his independence to the craving that has dominion over him. He is at the mercy of a compulsive desire that he is unable to resist.

Drugs create an irresistible dependency on the user. Drug abuse has created crisis in families and in our societies. Satan is pleased when a man is addicted to a chemical substance because addiction provides an easy mechanism for demonic control. There is always an underlying reason such as rejection, trauma, stress, and oppression that feeds an addiction. These reasons must seriously be addressed and confronted by the power and wisdom of God. If you have been ensnared by an addiction and have been in many programs without success, then now, is the time to come to Jesus Christ. The Bible says in John 8:36 that if Christ sets you free, you will truly be free. This means that the power of God will release you from every urge to fulfill your addictive desires. Thus, you will no longer be bound and drained by a spirit of addiction. However, a victim of addiction must be determined to be free. He must be disgusted by his addictive habit and by the factors that drive the addiction. You cannot love your addiction and seek deliverance from it at the same time. The more one feeds an addiction, the more entangled he becomes by it.

Sexual bondage and addiction to sex can manifest even without any act of sexual intercourse. Many are addicted to pornography, masturbation, and fantasizing (sexual thoughts). Thinking about alcohol does not make a person drunk. But thinking about sex can make a person fulfill a sexual need or lust.

But I say unto you, That whosoever looketh on a woman to lust after her hath committed adultery with her already in his heart. Matthew 5:28.

The modern world is fascinated and entrapped in a culture of sexual perversion and all manner of promiscuity. This is also evident in today's fashion that encourages all manner of seductive styles of dressing. The effect of this culture is to heighten lust in the population. Lust is a strong desire to fulfil a carnal need. The stronghold of sexual perversion has permeated cultures and we hear of allegations of sexual misconduct against our political and spiritual leaders that were hitherto unheard of. These allegations have brought mistrust and divisions in our communities and put a question mark on leadership. The Bible makes it clear that the only way to overcome lust is to walk in the Spirit (Galatians 5:16-17). Again, it takes the power of Jesus Christ to deliver one from lust and the spirit of lust that drive people to engage in sexual perversion as a lifestyle.

Waiting On the Lord

During a crisis, regardless of the circumstances, you must wait on the Lord for further instructions and clarification. You do not complain or begin to take matters into your own hands. If you go ahead of God, instead of waiting on Him, you will invite more trouble into your life. Running ahead of God is disobedience. Doing the right thing at the time not appointed by God is also tantamount to disobedience. It is futile to go ahead of God's presence. Be in His presence.

Wait for the Lord; be strong and take heart and wait for the Lord. Psalm 27:14.

But you must return to your God; maintain love and justice, and wait for your God always. Hosea 12:6.

God is Omnipotent and thus has the power to change your circumstances. He however desires that you wait for His will at His own timing. You must wait on Him despite the urge to move forward. In crisis, you must cultivate the practice of waiting with expectation for God to move. In our waiting, God uses the time to mold our character and prepare us for the expected manifestation.

As you wait on the Lord with the right attitude, God releases His peace and a sense of joy to flood your heart. And before you realize it, you are transitioning out of that crisis.

Prayers Against Satanic Oppression

1. Heavenly Father, in the name of Jesus Christ, I repent of all sins and ask for Your forgiveness.

2. I bind every power that has bound me and command them to release me now by fire in the name of Jesus.

3. I break every satanic chain of affliction upon my life in the name of Jesus.

4. I bind every strong man assigned and operating against me in the name of Jesus.

5. In the name of Jesus, I dismantle, disorganize, and destroy every demonic network and satanic conspiracy against my life with the blood of Jesus.

6. In the name of Jesus, I destroy and render powerless by the consuming fire of God, every household wickedness and familiar spirit that wants to keep me in perpetual crisis.

7. I reject every satanic alternative and counsel for my life in the name of Jesus.

8. Let the consuming fire of God destroy every destiny devourer assigned against my life in the mighty name of Jesus.

9. By the covenant power in the blood of Jesus, I overcome every destiny killer working against my life and command all destiny killers out of my life now in the name of Jesus.

10. I reject every sickness projected into my life by witch-craft powers and command every affliction of infirmity to return to their evil senders in Jesus name.

11. Heavenly Father, release angels to set me free from satanic oppression through government agencies and institutions of men in the name of Jesus.

12. O God, arise and scatter every strange power denying the manifestation of Your promises in my life and destroy their works against me in Jesus' name.

13. In the name of Jesus and by the anointing, I break and release myself from all yokes of failure, and frustration.

14. In the name of Jesus, I break any curse upon my life that demands that I be below and never above.

15. In the name of Jesus, I shall not live according to the set agenda of any evil strong man or ruler of darkness.

16. By my act of confession, repentance, and receiving forgiveness, I command in the name of Jesus that every spirit of lust and sexual perversion in my life be bound and cast out.

17. In the name of Jesus, I ask that the consuming fire of the Holy Spirit enter me and burn to ashes every unholy appetite and desire for illicit sexual activity.

18. In the mighty name of Jesus Christ, I come against every evil spirit enforcing the perpetuation of

addictive behaviors in my life. I bind such spirits and cast them out of my life in the name of Jesus.

19. In the name of Jesus, I renounce every idolatry of my ancestors and renounce all covenants with idols.

CHAPTER FOUR

Exiting Out of Toxic Relationships and Associations

A relationship can be viewed as a state in which one or more persons are connected or act toward one another. The Bible warns us about the company we are to keep. God forbade the Israelites from relating to certain nations because those nations would become a snare to them. Those nations eventually led Israel into idolatry.

Do not be misled: "Bad company corrupts good character." 1 Corinthians 15:33.

As children of God, we are called not to fellowship with darkness. Light and darkness have nothing in common.

14 Do not be yoked together with unbelievers. For what do righteousness and wickedness have in common? Or what fellowship can light have

with darkness? ¹⁵ What harmony is there between Christ and Belial? Or what does a believer have in common with an unbeliever? ¹⁶ What agreement is there between the temple of God and idols? For we are the temple of the living God. As God has said: "I will live with them and walk among them, and I will be their God, and they will be my people." ¹⁷ Therefore, "Come out from them and be separate, says the Lord. Touch no unclean thing, and I will receive you." ¹⁸ And, "I will be a Father to you, and you will be my sons and daughters, says the Lord Almighty." 2 Corinthians 6:14-18.

God does not approve of you being in a relationship that promotes the agenda of darkness at the expense of light. A relationship where God is not glorified is nothing but a toxic relationship. When you hang out with people that do not share the same quality of spiritual values that you have, you open the door for ungodly influences to enter your life. You are expected to relate with ungodly persons but not to the extent that you make a commitment to them in a relationship.

Some Effects of Toxic Relationships

1. Death

Deuteronomy 22:10 instructs us not to plow with an ox and a donkey yoked together. The donkey more than likely will influence the ox, a very hard worker to become playful. This was the case with Israel when they mingled with the nations. On their way to the promised land, the men of Israel began to mingle with Moabite women and committed fornication with them (Numbers 25). This resulted in the death by plague of 24,000 Israelites. Toxic relationships eventually lead to death if not dealt with promptly: death of the good that could have been; death of destiny.

2. Backsliding

King Solomon, however, loved many foreign women besides Pharaoh's daughter — Moabites, Ammonites, Edomites, Sidonians and Hittites. [2] They were from nations about which the Lord had told the Israelites, "You must not intermarry with them, because they will surely turn your hearts after their gods." Nevertheless, Solomon held fast to them in love. [3] He had seven hundred wives of royal birth and three hundred concubines, and his wives led him astray. [4] As Solomon grew old, his wives turned his heart after other gods, and his heart was not fully devoted to the Lord his God, as the heart of David his father had been. [5] He followed Ashtoreth the goddess of the Sidonians, and Molek the detestable god of the Ammonites. [6] So Solomon did evil in the eyes of the Lord; he did not follow the Lord completely, as David his father had done. 1 Kings 11:1-6.

King Solomon, a man that was blessed with so much wisdom by God, backslid because of his involvement in toxic relationships with women that worshipped strange gods. One effect of being in a toxic relationship is that it induces backsliding. Backsliding is growing cold and leaving our first love, Jesus Christ.

3. Isolation

Toxic relationships have a way of striving against every healthy relationship to gain dominance. For instance, the person in an abusive and controlling relationship will keep that relationship away from every other relationship. With time, the abusive, controlling relationship will begin to demand more time and more space from other relationships. Joseph found himself in a relationship where his brothers were so envious of him that they sold him into bondage in Egypt. The toxic relationship Joseph had with his brothers eventually deprived him of the healthy relationship he had with his father, Jacob. Joseph's brothers isolated him by making him a slave, but God distinguished Joseph from his brothers by making him second to Pharaoh. The Bible in Genesis 49:26 refers to Joseph thus:

> The blessings of thy father have prevailed above the blessings of my progenitors unto the utmost bound of the everlasting hills: they shall be on the head of Joseph, and on the crown of the head of him that was separate from his brethren.

When you are in a relationship where the other party is not pleased with you excelling, that is a toxic relationship. In a relationship where the other party is envious of favor or status (coat of many colors) bestowed upon you, that is a toxic relationship.

4. Stress and Fatigue

In the book of Judges 16, we see Samson jump from one toxic relationship to another. Samson finds himself in a relationship with a woman named Delilah. Samson fell in love with Delilah, a woman that owed allegiance to Samson's enemies. Delilah kept nagging Samson to reveal to her the source of his strength. Eventually, Samson yielded to the stress of Delilah's prodding. Samson opened the door of his heart to a woman that had no business being near him in the first place. This toxic relationship with Delilah resulted in Samson losing not only his strength but his vision. Be cautious not to enter a relationship that will dissipate your strength and leave you burnt out. Some through being in the wrong relationship have deviated from the vision that God had for them. The relationship has drained them and limited them from accomplishing all that God desired for them.

Unprofitable Associations

There are other toxic relationships that are fostered by memberships in certain associations, clubs, and organizations. Some groups exist to promote social welfare and justice. While these are desirable, care must be taken to ensure that they are not given preeminence over our Christian obligations to our home and our local church.

There are some other groups that are just outright ungodly and must be avoided. Examples of these are Free Masonry, Eastern Star, and other similar lodges.

If you are in a social club that demands more time and resources from you than you give to God, then that social club is not profitable. Things that are lawful may not necessarily be helpful. A legitimate association may also have the potential to diminish you spiritually.

Exiting a Toxic Relationship

It is important that you pray before allowing anyone or group of persons have entry into your life because once you yield space, it is difficult to take it back without hurting feelings. This was a problem that Samson always seemed to face: being in toxic relationships. Samson allowed persons like Delilah that had no business being in his life occupy valuable space that eventually resulted in his downfall (Judges16). Eventually, because of the space that Samson had allowed Delilah to occupy in his life, Delilah became instrumental in facilitating Samson's downfall. Samson lacked the will to exit from a toxic relationship.

Exiting a toxic relationship will demand that soul ties be broken. You must ask God for grace, courage, and wisdom because you will most likely encounter severe resistance and pressure as you turn your back to these toxic relationships. In some of these relationships, you may have shared your secrets with others, and you may have even shared your life with others. Your removing yourself from the relationship may result in confidences and trusts being broken. You will have to pray to God to minimize the backlash and give you the grace to endure the consequences of exiting from a toxic relationship.

Depending on the relationship, you may have to do a gradual departure or an immediate departure.

In 2 Corinthians 6, the Word of God instructs us to have no fellowship with darkness and to come out from relationships that glorify darkness and that God will receive us for doing so. This means that the power of God will be available to you as you leave these toxic relationships.

At times, when you want to leave a bad relationship, there may be overt and subtle threats directed at you. There are relationships and associations where blood covenants were entered into that demand grave consequences if one decides to leave. These evil covenants are structured this way to discourage a person from leaving the group or the relationship. In such situations, you must plead the blood of Jesus to cover you from the agenda of retaliation.

When the children of Israel sought to leave Egypt, Egypt resisted them and put all manner of obstacles in their way. Egypt did not want to let go of a benefit they were receiving. Egypt sought to continue exploiting the nation of Israel. In similar fashion, the spirit of bondage always resists the deliverance of God's people. On the night of Passover, the blood was applied, and Israel was released. In the same way, you shall plead the blood of Jesus and see your release.

When Israel went out of Egypt, the house of Jacob from a people of strange language; Judah was his sanctuary, and Israel his dominion. Psalm 114:1-2.

Israel had to come out of Egypt. So long as Israel was in Egypt under the yoke of Pharaoh, they were in crisis. Israel had to come out of a people of strange language. When you are connected to a people of strange language, you cannot understand them, and they cannot understand you. Your demands will not make sense to them and their demands will not make sense to you anymore, if it did previously. It is after Israel came out of Egypt that we see Judah become the Lord's sanctuary and Israel his dominion. Israel had come out of Egypt, but it was apparent that Egypt had not come out of Israel. After leaving Egypt, Israel continued to exhibit a longing for the things of Egypt and demonstrated Egyptian traits such as idolatry.

Relationships have consequences because they involve exchanges. In a relationship, there are things you receive and things you give. There are things that leave you and things that enter you. Because of a relationship, a person can be infested with lust, bitterness, anger, resentment, and unforgiveness. You must be careful that when you transition out of a toxic relationship, you leave all its toxic properties behind. If you carry the properties of a toxic relationship such as bitterness with you, you have not successfully transitioned out of that relationship. That relationship still lives inside you. The longer one remains in a toxic relationship, the more susceptible he may become to demonic strongholds. Thought patterns and feelings are influenced by the degree of involvement and experiences one has in certain types of relationships.

For example, a woman who has belonged to a feminist movement that attacks the authority of the man in the family may have built up, a stronghold that devalues men. This stronghold will eventually play out in her marriage until it is acknowledged and dealt with. For her marriage to succeed, she must cut off all the so-called support she receives from that feminist movement. She must severe soul ties with members of that movement. Furthermore, she must seek deliverance from every mental and spiritual stronghold that has been consolidated in her through this toxic relationship she is now renouncing.

Exiting Out of Occult and Secret Societies

Secret societies instill fear in their members. When a member decides to leave, one of his major battles will be with fear. Evil spirits will be assigned to cause fear and panic in him or her and to ensure that the person is kept in perpetual bondage. Fear paralyzes one from making rational decisions and induces double-mindedness. A young man in his early thirties came for one of our deliverance services in Brooklyn, New York. He had driven for roughly 5 hours from Rochester, New York. He sought to get out of an occult group that dealt with the Sango deity. He demonstrated fear and double-mindedness. We pointed him to the cross of Jesus Christ. He was not fully willing to renounce his occult society but, yet he wanted deliverance from the spirits that were tormenting him.

As we began to pray with him, the demons in him manifested violently and our team of ministers had to physically restrain him. We got him to renounce Satan and all the works and spirits of his occult society. He renounced them with a degree of reluctance that one can only pray that he received complete freedom. A person that wants deliverance from the occult must express no reluctance or hesitation. He must have his mind made up and must be determined to resist the manipulations of the enemy. He cannot afford to be double-minded.

> If any of you lack wisdom, let him ask of God, that giveth to all men liberally, and upbraideth not; and it shall be given him. But let him ask in faith, nothing wavering. For he that wavereth is like a wave of the sea driven with the wind and tossed. For let not that man think that he shall receive any thing of the Lord. A double minded man is unstable in all his ways.

The book of James 1:7-8 says that a double minded man is unstable in all his ways and cannot receive anything of the Lord. Deliverance is a thing of the Lord. Deliverance is not for the double-minded.

Initiation into the realm of the occult brings a person into a legal contract with Satan. For deliverance to occur, that contract and the legal rights it conferred on satanic powers must be broken and destroyed. In this area, deliverance is hardly a one-time event. Counseling and healing must be ministered to the one being delivered. He must be discipled thoroughly in Christ and encouraged to die to self daily (deny himself) on the cross (Luke 9:23). The process of deliverance involves sanctification, crucifying the flesh, and resisting sin. The person must not willingly succumb to sin or the occult powers will retain dominion over him.

In addition, exiting from the occult and seeking deliverance demands that all objects of the occult be destroyed as God prescribed: by burning them in fire. In 2015, I had gone to a young man's house in Queens, New York in the company of two workers in our ministry. The young man had renounced Free Masonry and was actively seeking deliverance. We collected all his occult paraphernalia, including ceremonial garments and a satanic bible, and burnt them in fire in his backyard. The fire let out a strange smoke as we prayed continually for his deliverance and praised God. You cannot turn your back on the devil and keep his property. You must burn them to destruction. As we were burning these items, the question arose as to what to do with other occult objects that did not belong to him and that he had to return to the occult lodge. He was advised that if the owners could not pick them up by the next day, then they must also be destroyed. Getting out of Satan's territory is often a painstaking exercise.

In a nut shell, deliverance from the occult involves:

1. Confession
2. Repentance
3. Forgiveness

4. Renunciation of evil covenants
5. Breaking of soul ties with occult members and occult spirits
6. Fasting and Prayer
7. Binding the strong man and casting out demons
8. Healing
9. Counselling
10. Obedience
11. Walking in Faith

Marriage and Divorce

The essence of marriage is to make man and woman happy and to bring out the best in them. Many have entered marriage on the assumption that it will solve their problems, only to discover otherwise. A marriage cannot make up for a deficiency in the character of one or both partners. When there is tension in a marriage, it is important to address the issues from the root. Most times, the problem is not understood until there is an appreciation of what drives a spouse to act the way he or she does. Major roots that threaten marriages include insecurity, rejection, bitterness, fear, lust, and anger. Until these demonic hindrances are addressed and uprooted, it will be almost impossible to have a healthy marriage. In addition, many marriages experience difficulties because the spouses are unequally yoked. Such marriages begin on a very weak foundation and the devil is quick to ensure that the marriage never progresses.

Satan will fight against your determination to remain in your marriage, and you must submit to God and resist him. If you are ignorant of the devil's devices, it will be very hard for you to stay in your marriage and enjoy it. Marriage could be a very heavy burden to bear. In such instances, the spouses must remember to adhere to their vows of staying together, for better, for worse, till death do them part.

Can two walk together, except they be agreed? Amos 3:3.

For Christian marriages to be strong and prosperous, spouses must learn to agree with each other in the spirit of sacrificial love. We must learn to often displease ourselves in order to please our spouses. If a marriage has irretrievably broken down, and has become a theatre of incessant oppression and conflict, a separation for a season is strongly advised. In the period of separation, both spouses must be willing to work on themselves. They should seek godly counsel and be willing to submit to godly counsel.

The divorce rate has increased dramatically in western societies to the point that many are discouraged from ever considering marriage. The aftermath of a divorce invariably leads to crisis. Children of the marriage will begin to experience insecurities and vulnerabilities they were shielded from in a united home. Litigation for child support, custody, and dissolution of marital property often creates animosity between the two that once professed undying love for one another. Divorcees must ensure that they do not transfer the anger and bitterness flowing from their divorce into the lives of their children. Children, as much as possible, must be shielded from the drama of a divorce so that they do not grow up scarred with a tendency to repeat the sins of their parents.

Marriage brings two flesh to become one. Divorce separates the one flesh back into two. This comes with emotional pain and financial loss. Divorce affects the soul and time is needed to bring healing. Until the divorced spouse is willing to forgive the other spouse, they cannot experience healing and deliverance from the toxic marriage.

When a Toxic Relationship Releases You

Sometimes, it is the toxic relationship that will release you for reasons best known to that relationship. When a toxic person releases an individual, that individual may feel vulnerable especially if he was dependent upon the resources, affirmation, and company of that toxic relationship. It is at such a time that you must learn to depend on God for provision and sustenance. You must move your trust from man to God. When a toxic person or group releases you, you must learn to release yourself. Discard feelings of rejection, and insecurity and immediately begin to build a safety wall between you and the toxic person or group.

Exiting Other Relationships

On the other hand, there are some relationships from the past that are not necessarily toxic. However, they are just the kind of relationships that have outlived their usefulness. You have grown beyond the relationship. You will also need to transition from such a relationship so that it does not drain and impede you. You may not need to cut that relationship off, but you will need to spend less time and resources nurturing that relationship. Divine wisdom is needed to know what level of priority to accord to such relationships.

Prayers of Deliverance from the Occult

1. I present my entire being unto the Lord as a living sacrifice for cleansing through the blood of Jesus. In the name of Jesus, let the blood of Jesus cleanse me from every sin, curse, evil covenant, ungodly soul tie, and guilt.

2. In the name of Jesus Christ, I cancel, renounce, and reverse every occult initiation, dedication, and projection upon my life.

3. I break the power of every occult authority, occult altar, and occult manifestation over my life in the name of Jesus Christ.

4. In the name of Jesus Christ and by the power of the Holy Spirit, I release myself from every blood covenant that connects me to the realm of the occult.

5. I break every occult curse against my life in the name of Jesus.

6. Every legal ground that occult spirits have in my life, be destroyed by the overcoming power in the blood of Jesus.

7. Heavenly Father, place a hedge of protection around me and send fierce warrior angels to guard me against demonic infiltration and attacks in the name of Jesus.

8. In the name of Jesus, I trample upon and destroy every serpent and scorpion and all the power of the enemy that has been opposing my progress.

9. In the name of Jesus Christ, I receive deliverance from every demonic induced crisis and bind all demonic powers assigned to impose a regime of crisis upon my life.

10. I plead the blood of Jesus against spiritual forces of wickedness in high places that are conspiring to keep me in the same spot.

Prayers of Deliverance from Toxic Relationships

11. In the name of Jesus, I forgive all that hurt or betrayed me in past relationships and pray the Lord's salvation upon them.

12. I renounce and break, in the name of Jesus, every covenant I made apart from God that ties me to a being that is unwilling to let go.

13. In the name of Jesus and by the power in the blood of Jesus, I break every evil soul tie I have with past sexual partners through sexual sin.

14. Heavenly Father, let there be an uncontestable severance of evil soul ties between me and any anyone that You do not approve of, in the name of Jesus.

15. In the name of Jesus, I bind the strong man assigned to destroy my marriage and destroy all his evil works by the power in the blood of Jesus.

16. Lord Jesus, I repent of every sin that I have committed against my marriage vows and ask of Your forgiveness.

17. I reject every satanic alternative and counsel for my marriage in the name of Jesus.

18. Heavenly Father, put a hedge of protection around my marriage and keep demonic interference out in Jesus' name.

19. Heavenly Father, in the name of Jesus, let those that are tied to me through evil covenant, lose interest in my matter and forsake their evil ways.

20. In the name of Jesus, let the blood of Jesus separate me from every demonic power that has access into my life because of any past relationship.

CHAPTER FIVE

Spiritual Approach to Financial Crisis

Wisdom is the principal thing; therefore get wisdom: and with all thy getting get understanding. Proverbs 4:7.

Through wisdom is an house builded; and by understanding it is established: And by knowledge shall the chambers be filled with all precious and pleasant riches. Proverbs 24:3-4.

If any of you lack wisdom, let him ask of God, that giveth to all men liberally, and upbraideth not; and it shall be given him. James 1:5.

No man is an island. Man must relate to one another and form relationships that will enable them reach the apex of their destiny. Man is interdependent on his fellow man and his success will depend on how he relates with others. In life, you must cherish your total dependence on God and God alone. In Luke 15, Jesus tells the parable of the prodigal son. His rise, fall and rise is clearly seen in the choices he made and how he related to God and to his fellow man.

> [10] Likewise, I say unto you, there is joy in the presence of the angels of God over one sinner that repenteth. [11] And he said, A certain man had two sons:[12] And the younger of them said to his father, Father, give me the portion of goods that falleth to me. And he divided unto them his living. [13] And not many days after the younger son gathered all together, and took his journey into a far country, and there wasted his substance with riotous living. [14] And when he had spent all, there arose a mighty famine in that land; and he began to be in want. [15] And he went and joined himself to a citizen of that country; and he sent him into his fields to feed swine. [16] And he would fain have filled his belly with the husks that the swine did eat: and no man gave unto him. [17] And when he came to himself, he said, How many hired servants of my father's have bread enough and to spare, and I perish with hunger! [18] I will arise and go to my father, and will say unto him, Father, I have sinned against heaven, and before thee, [19] And am no more worthy to be called thy son: make me as one of thy hired servants. [20] And he arose, and came to his father. But when he was yet a great way off, his father saw

him, and had compassion, and ran, and fell on his neck, and kissed him. [21] And the son said unto him, Father, I have sinned against heaven, and in thy sight, and am no more worthy to be called thy son. [22] But the father said to his servants, Bring forth the best robe, and put it on him; and put a ring on his hand, and shoes on his feet: [23] And bring hither the fatted calf, and kill it; and let us eat, and be merry: [24] For this my son was dead, and is alive again; he was lost, and is found. And they began to be merry. [25] Now his elder son was in the field: and as he came and drew nigh to the house, he heard musick and dancing. [26] And he called one of the servants, and asked what these things meant. [27] And he said unto him, Thy brother is come; and thy father hath killed the fatted calf, because he hath received him safe and sound. [28] And he was angry, and would not go in: therefore came his father out, and intreated him. [29] And he answering said to his father, Lo, these many years do I serve thee, neither transgressed I at any time thy commandment: and yet thou never gavest me a kid, that I might make merry with my friends: [30] But as soon as this thy son was come, which hath devoured thy living with harlots, thou hast killed for him the fatted calf. [31] And he said unto him, Son, thou art ever with me, and all that I have is thine. [32] It was meet that we should make merry, and be glad: for this thy brother was dead, and is alive again; and was lost, and is found.

There are a few lessons we can quickly learn from the above-mentioned story. The younger son lived recklessly and foolishly and so squandered his great fortune he had received from his father. Because he did not invest his funds, his funds were quickly depleted, and he entered a financial crisis. In this crisis, he was now reduced to about the lowest form of servitude and deprivation. The turning point in his crisis was when he made up his mind to make a drastic change by returning to his father's house. One of the roots of his problem was that he left his father's house prematurely. To make this drastic change, the prodigal son had to humble himself. The Bible says that he came to his senses. If you want to come out of a pit, the first thing you do is to stop digging. If you are overwhelmed by credit card debt, the first thing you do is to curtail your spending. You must come to your senses. Upon his repentance of riotous living and his return to his father's house, he was restored to his prosperity to the chagrin of his elder brother. Do not be surprised that when you experience a financial increase that some people close to you will express irritation and be vexed in spirit.

Many have acted like the prodigal son did initially. God had given them resources and they had squandered it on frivolities and trivial pursuits. Others may have buried what God gave them to prosper with underneath the ground.

One of the first spiritual approaches you must develop in a financial crisis is that you must see yourself as a faithful steward of every resource (time, money, people, etc) that

God has placed in your hands. You cannot afford to be reckless and you must constantly ask God for wisdom. If you are in a rut, you must come to your senses and return to your Father's house that is filled with wisdom, knowledge, understanding, grace, and all manner of riches.

When the prodigal son first acquired his inheritance, he left for a faraway land. He went out of his father's reach and so was disconnected from the one that could have counselled and mentored him. In any crisis, make sure you get sound godly advice. Do not distance yourself from people that are skilled at financial planning and wealth building. Do not associate with people who enjoy a lifestyle of devouring fortunes and adding no value to your life. The prodigal spent his funds on prostitutes and partying: an investment that invites sudden poverty. Until the prodigal son re-connected to his father, he was bound to live the life of a destitute. Who do you need to reconnect with or connect to?

Networks and Connections

When you truly desire victory over your finances, you will take a stand against toxic relationships that suck your finances. Then, you will begin to develop connections that encourage you to live a life of purpose. A life of purpose ties loose ends, seals leaks, seeks opportunity for personal development so that it can accomplish that which it was created to do. Your inner circle must consist of individuals that are God-fearing, disciplined, and wise. In your inner circle must be individuals that can show you where to plant a seed to reap a good harvest. You must terminate barren and unproductive relationships that do not point you in the direction of freedom.

In 2 Samuel 9 we see the case of a man named Mephibosheth, who ended up in a barren place called Lo Debar through no fault of his.

> And David said, Is there yet any that is left of the house of Saul, that I may shew him kindness for Jonathan's sake? ² And there was of the house of Saul a servant whose name was Ziba. And when they had called him unto David, the king said unto him, Art thou Ziba? And he said, Thy servant is he. ³ And the king said, Is there not yet any of the house of Saul, that I may shew the kindness of God unto him? And Ziba said unto the king, Jonathan hath yet a son, which is lame on his feet. ⁴ And the king said unto him, Where is he? And Ziba said unto the king, Behold, he is in the house of Machir, the son of Ammiel, in Lodebar. ⁵ Then king David sent, and fetched him out of the house of Machir, the son of Ammiel, from Lodebar. ⁶ Now when Mephibosheth, the son of Jonathan, the son of Saul, was come unto David, he fell on his face, and did reverence. And David said, Mephibosheth. And he answered, Behold thy servant! ⁷ And David said unto him, Fear not: for I will surely shew thee kindness for Jonathan thy father's sake, and will restore thee all the land of Saul thy father; and thou shalt eat bread at my table continually. ⁸ And he bowed himself,

and said, What is thy servant, that thou shouldest look upon such a dead dog as I am? [9] Then the king called to Ziba, Saul's servant, and said unto him, I have given unto thy master's son all that pertained to Saul and to all his house.

As a result of his being dropped by his nurse when he was a young boy, Mephibosheth became lame on both feet. Mephibosheth now became stuck in Lo Debar, a barren place that promises nothing. Poor Mephibosheth! Mephibosheth, the grandson of king Saul, grew up in royalty, yet life changed and worsened by his being dropped. The nurse that ought to look after him, dropped him accidentally. Many today have been dropped by people they thought would help them and consequently, have become financially lame. Lame people tend to often ask for handouts and become comfortable merely receiving handouts.

Who you associate with is very important. The voices in Lo Debar will try and keep you in Lo Debar. Do not listen to the voices of Lo Debar that want you to remain in your crisis. Lo Debar will not release you until you are ready to fight. A covenant fought for Mephibosheth. A covenant entered into between David and Jonathan spoke in favor of Mephibosheth. What is fighting for you? Who is interceding on your behalf? Who is advocating for you? Interestingly, Mephibosheth's change of circumstances for the better had nothing to do with his performance. All Mephibosheth had to do was say, "Yes," when king David called. In similar fashion, God is calling you to come out of Lo Debar into a higher place. The will of God is that you be fruitful and not barren.

Mephibosheth's help came not from within Lo Debar but from the king's palace. Mephibosheth needed to get unstuck. He was entangled by his lameness. You must get rid of every lameness, every weight that entangles you and that wants to keep you in a dry, barren wasteland. The religious spirit may be the one to tell a Mephibosheth to pray about David's offer. This spirit will keep a Mephibosheth entangled in prayer at the expense of his stepping out in faith.

Are you ready to come out of Lo Debar? You can be anointed and still be in Lo Debar. There are many anointed Christians in Lo Debar entrapped by their own perceived limitations. In 2 Samuel 9:8, Mephibosheth perceived himself as a dead dog. Why? Because in Lo Debar that is how people tend to see themselves. To prosper, while remaining humble, you must get rid of the Lo Debar mentality. It is a stronghold that wants to confine you to a minimal existence and then lie to you that your case has been written off and that there is no hope. When David sent for Mephibosheth, he could have said, "no." He had a choice (yes or no). Many Christians in Lo Debar also have a choice. Some like Lo Debar because Lo Debar satisfies them with liquor stores, night clubs and empty promises that makes them forget their life purpose. Do not get comfortable in your Lo Debar. Get out of Lo Debar! You can do all things through Christ that strengthens you (Philippians 4:13).

Lo Debar not only represents a spiritual place, it represents a geographical location. Some will have to relocate from their current physical location to see progress. If you are in an environment that undermines and depreciates your value, then you will have to take steps not to be subject to that environment and its powers.

Diligently Seek God

But without faith it is impossible to please him: for he that cometh to God must believe that he is, and that he is a rewarder of them that diligently seek him. Hebrews 11:6.

Faith is an absolute necessity. It is the key to living a life that pleases God. God was so pleased with the faith of Abraham that He credited it to Abraham as righteousness. Faith believes not only in the existence of God but believes in God and the Word of God. Even the devils believe that there is God but that does not count as faith. Genuine faith believes and submits to the Word of God. Faith seeks God diligently. You cannot come to God unless you first believe that He is. God rewards those with a living faith that seek Him diligently. He will reward you even if you find yourself in a pit or prison like Joseph was. He will honor you and cause you to prosper.

When you set aside time to seek God diligently, do not be distracted by people, activities, or your situation. You must set aside time exclusively for God. You must set this time aside to seek God in prayer, in fasting, and in His Word. God must have the pre-eminence in your life. Your diligently seeking God demands that God comes before every other person and everything in your life. You must be hungry and thirsty for God. Merely attending church services is not diligently seeking God. Cultivate a lifestyle of spending time alone with God in prayer and in the Bible. Tell Him how much you love, appreciate, and believe in Him. He will begin to pour into you His wisdom to solve complex life problems and to move ahead.

You must make it your goal to please God. True faith that trusts the Word of God will not violate the Word of God. Faith obeys the Word. God rewards the faith that obeys the Word of God. God will reward you with your heart desire and will stand with you in the difficulties of life.

2 Chronicles 26 narrates how God made king Uzziah prosper as long as he sought the Lord. There is a connection between living a godly life and prospering. As soon as king Uzziah became strong, he grew proud, and disregarded God, to his own destruction. When you diligently continuously seek God, God will restrain the devourers that deplete your resources. He will give you wisdom in terms of how to preserve and grow your finances. If you seek worldliness and the pleasures of the world, just remember that they are fleeting and do not truly satisfy. Seek first the kingdom of God and His righteousness and all other things shall be added unto you (Matthew 6:33). In the kingdom of God is peace and joy. These two ingredients are needed in a financial crisis. You cannot allow yourself to be a bitter person because of your financial status.

Neither can you allow yourself to become proud because of your financial status. You must learn to be content while aspiring for more.

It is also important to understand God's will amid a financial trial. God's will is that you prosper and be in good health. Yet, God may take you through a pruning and purging to position you to bear much fruit. Do not be discouraged if you come upon times of financial difficulties. Stand on God's word that reassures that God knows the thoughts that he thinks towards you, thoughts of peace, and not of evil, to give you an expected end (Jeremiah 29:11).

The Laws of Sowing and Reaping

Except you are depending on the goodwill of others, which could be very frustrating, you will never reap a harvest until you plant a seed. You must invest something (time, money) in order to see a yield. The main question that arises is what to invest and where to invest it. Many will try and convince you to invest in their enterprise or ministry, but you must understand why you are investing where you are investing. There has been lots of abuse in the area of sowing and reaping. Proponents of the prosperity gospel have often claimed that when one sows financially into their ministries, that one will receive a miracle. These unverified claims have only succeeded in fueling the spirit of greed and caused so much reproach to the name of Christ.

The first thing to understand is that planting a seed in faith does not necessarily guarantee a great harvest. Certain factors, such as the quality of the soil, may work against a harvest. If you plant a viable seed (time and money) in a barren soil (enterprise, ministry, etc.) you will not experience the desired fruitfulness. All such soil will give you is barrenness.

> In the morning sow thy seed, and in the evening withhold not thy hand: for thou knowest not whether shall prosper, either this or that, or whether they both shall be alike good. Ecclesiastes 11:6.

The best time to sow thy seed is in the morning. Do not procrastinate. The earlier you take steps to get out of a crisis the better for you. The earlier you put a stop to unnecessary expenses, the better. If you are determined to plant a good seed, also be determined to remove all the weed that are waiting to choke your seed. The weed includes the discouragers, mockers, and negative attitudes that may be in you.

In 2 Kings 4, all a poor widow had was a little oil and she was willing to release it to the prophet Elisha and follow his instructions. She got all the empty jars she could find and filled them up with the little oil that she had. If there was an empty jar, there was enough oil to fill it up. The widow was able to sell the jars of oil and pay off all her debts. The widow's faith and willingness to obey the spoken word of God broke the yoke of debt off her life. In similar fashion, you must listen to the right godly counsel from a true man of God.

It is not by being stingy that one prospers. It is more blessed to give than it is to receive. The Bible says that when you are kind to the poor, you are lending to God and the Lord will reward you for your generosity (Proverbs 19:17).

> Give, and it shall be given unto you; good measure, pressed down, and shaken together, and running over, shall men give into your bosom. For with the same measure that ye mete withal it shall be measured to you again. Luke 6:38.

The word of God in Luke 6:38 is saying that how you give will determine how you will receive and that what you give, will determine what you will receive. Be faithful in your giving. To the faithful, God shows Himself faithful (Psalm 18:25). As you are faithful in your giving (kindness, which is a fruit of the Spirit), God will be faithful in ensuring that you receive.

These truths mentioned above are gospel truths which some have sought to exploit and abuse to the detriment of the undiscerning. You cannot buy a miracle, an anointing, or a financial breakthrough. Prospering financially goes beyond merely sowing a seed. It calls for you to be educated in your area of work, to be disciplined, to be a good student, exercise faith, and much more. Merely sowing a seed (investing time and money) without being disciplined will not take you out of the valleys.

Tithes and Offerings

The New Testament did not abolish the tithes and offerings as some have suggested. Tithing was established prior to the Mosaic Law when Abraham gave a tenth of his war spoils to Melchizedek in Genesis 14 (the king of Righteousness, Priest of God Most High, Christ pre-incarnate). Tithing is an act of worship and it precedes the old testament laws. In Malachi 3, God makes it clear that the tithes are His property and that His people were robbing Him of what was due Him.

> Will a man rob God? Yet ye have robbed me. But ye say, Wherein have we robbed thee? In tithes and offerings. Ye are cursed with a curse: for ye have robbed me, even this whole nation. Bring ye all the tithes into the storehouse, that there may be meat in mine house, and prove me now herewith, saith the Lord of hosts, if I will not open you the windows of heaven, and pour you out a blessing, that there shall not be room enough to receive it. And I will rebuke the devourer for your sakes, and he shall not destroy the fruits of your ground; neither shall your vine cast her fruit before the time in the field, saith the Lord of hosts. And all nations shall call you blessed: for ye shall be a delightsome land, saith the Lord of hosts. Malachi 3:8-12.

The tithes and offerings belong to God. To use them or misappropriate them for personal gain is tantamount to robbing God. Robbing God of tithes and offerings brings a curse and opens the door for the devourer to plunder your expectations.

Even though paying tithes to God was done before the Law, it was approved under Grace in the New Testament.

> Woe unto you, scribes and Pharisees, hypocrites! For ye pay tithes of mint and anise and cumin, and have omitted the weightier matters of the law, judgment, mercy, and faith: these ought ye to have done, and not to leave the other undone. Matthew 23:23.

As a believer, when you pay tithes to the Lord, you honor God and help build the kingdom. Those in positions of authority in the house of God that abuse the Lord's tithe will answer to the Lord on the day of reckoning.

Discipline and Character

The character of a believer must reflect the person of Christ. You will need the mind of Christ to overcome the temptations that lead to the downfall and financial irrelevance of a man. This is what was initially lacking in the prodigal son. His character was one wholly defined by self-indulgence. When you are Christ-centered as opposed to self-centered, you minimize the temptations of the pitfalls desperately waiting to consume you.

To build and manage wealth requires discipline and strength of character. In the parable of the shrewd manager (Luke 16:1-13), Jesus tells the story of the shrewd manager who was about to be fired for squandering his master's property. The manager gave his master's debtors a discount and thus won favor from them. The master commended the manager for his cleverness. In the NIV, Luke 16:8-9 reads:

> The master commended the dishonest manager because he had acted shrewdly. For the people of this world are more shrewd in dealing with their own kind than are the people of the light. I tell you, use worldly wealth to gain friends for yourself, so that when it is gone, you will be welcomed into eternal dwellings.

Jesus acknowledged in this parable that the people of the world are shrewder than believers. Believers can learn from the people of the world without compromising and copying their behavior. Christ admonishes us to use money in such a way that we demonstrate friendship and the love of Christ (kindness, compassion) to others so that at the end, you enjoy eternal rewards. Sometimes a simple gift, given in love, (not a bribe!) will open great doors for you.

In the case of Joseph in the book of Genesis, he was quite shrewd in building wealth for the house of Pharaoh. Joseph understood the economics of the famine that hit Egypt and, so he was able to profit from it. In Genesis 47, Joseph received all the moneys, livestock, and lands of the Egyptians in exchange for food. Joseph increased Pharaoh's assets in the time of severe famine. The Egyptians were reduced to servitude under Joseph's leadership. Joseph, a slave boy in Egypt, grew to the most prominent position in Egypt besides Pharaoh because of his strength of character and his demonstration of wisdom, knowledge, and understanding.

Discipline is most essential when seeking to grow financially. You must avoid traits like slothfulness and procrastination. You must avoid spending your day on social media or television. You must spend more time on those things that have the capacity to build wealth and character. Developing the right character demands self-control and self-discipline. It calls for practicing delayed gratification until certain financial milestones are reached. It calls for developing a budget and honoring it. A budget should encourage you to commit to spending less than what you earn.

If discipline proves to be a challenge for you, then it is best to seek out a mentor that you can be accountable to. Be accountable to a person that is financially independent and stable. Your mentor must be someone that can speak positively into your life situations and a person you can look up to for guidance and direction.

Financial Breakthrough Often Requires Spiritual Warfare

Getting out of a financial crisis such as loss of income, rising debt and inability to meet financial obligations will in addition require that you engage in spiritual warfare. There are certain chronic financial problems that are caused by strange spiritual forces or that are taken advantage of by such forces. Satanic powers are adept at imposing and enforcing curses of poverty, failure, limitation, stagnation, frustration, and delay in the lives of their victims. A curse is an evil pronouncement that is often enforced by a strongman and network of demons. Until such curses and spells are broken and destroyed, it will be difficult to experience meaningful financial progress. There are some that are very hard working and disciplined yet have no fruit to show for all their hard work and discipline. This may invariably be because of the workings of invisible demonic powers that have been given the assignment to frustrate their efforts.

The Bible talks about binding the strong man. Therefore, it is of importance that you know who the strong man is in every situation. The strong man has a house and he guards it fiercely. In his house are his possessions, which he has appropriated from his victims over a considerable period of time. The strong man is an agent of Satan that delights in perpetuating misery in the lives of his victims. To be effective against the strong man in spiritual warfare, you must first bind him in the name of Jesus.

> When a strong man, fully armed, guards his own house, his possessions are safe. But when someone stronger attacks and overpowers him, he takes away the armor in which the man trusted and divides up the spoils. Luke 11:20-22.

When a demonic strong man has detained your blessings, you must contend against him in the spiritual realm in the mighty name of Jesus Christ.

What many are trusting God for is Restoration. The devil is a thief that comes to steal, kill, and destroy (John 10:10). You can be rest assured, in faith, that you will recover and be restored in the name of Jesus.

> ²⁴ Shall the prey be taken from the mighty, or the lawful captive delivered? ²⁵ But thus saith the LORD, Even the captives of the mighty shall be taken away, and the prey of the terrible shall be delivered: for I will contend with him that contendeth with thee, and I will save thy children. ²⁶ And I will feed them that oppress thee with their own flesh; and they shall be drunken with their own blood, as with sweet wine: and all flesh shall know that I the LORD am thy Savior and thy Redeemer, the mighty One of Jacob. Isaiah 49:24-26.

The Bible in Isaiah 49 refers to the strong man as "the mighty" and "the terrible." He is mighty, but he is not the Almighty. As strong as the strong man is, he can be bound. Once he is bound and cast out of a life, that life is assured of deliverance and must now take steps to enforce and maintain that deliverance. Maintaining deliverance requires steering clear off dangerous patterns of behavior and embracing the Word and the Spirit of God.

The spiritual approach you adopt towards a financial crisis will go a long way in determining how and when you will come out of it. In faith, begin to see yourself out of the pit, stop digging, and build a ladder to work your way out. Pray to the Lord for your speedy deliverance.

I called upon the Lord in distress: the Lord answered me, and set me in a large place. Psalm 118:5.

As you work on your discipline, pray unto the Lord in faith and get ready: the Lord is taking you to a larger place.

Prayers for Financial Breakthrough

1. Heavenly Father, if I have ever taken advantage of or exploited anyone financially, I repent of this sin in the name of Jesus. I ask for the grace to make restitution at the proper time, and ask for Your forgiveness in Jesus name.

2. Lord, in the name of Jesus, I repent for any time I did not show mercy to the poor when I had the means to help them.

3. In the name of Jesus, I repent for any time I withheld my tithes and offerings and ask that any curse associated with this sin be broken in Jesus' name.

4. In the name of Jesus, every enemy of my increase scatter and be destroyed by the consuming fire of God.

5. Every satanic power holding my prosperity, release it now unto me and die, in the name of Jesus.

6. In the name of Jesus Christ, I bind principalities and powers of darkness and command their agents by force to release my blessings and virtues.

7. In the name of Jesus Christ and by the power of the Holy Spirit, I command all evil devices, evil altars, and evil spirits detaining my blessings, my prosperity, my wealth, my health, and my breakthrough to release their grip and hold immediately.

8. Every spiritual Herod, Pharaoh, Goliath against my prosperity, I dethrone you and render you powerless in the name of Jesus.

9. Let every spiritual blockade to breakthrough in my life be consumed by the fire of God, in the name of Jesus.

10. O Lord, in the name of Jesus, let not my enemies triumph over me.

11. O Lord, promote me from minimum to maximum in Jesus' name.

12. Let any power storing my blessings in any body of water begin to release them unto me now in Jesus' name.

13. By the power of the Holy Spirit, I clear my goods from all satanic warehouses in the name of Jesus.

14. Let the angels conveying my blessings receive overcoming divine reinforcement in the name of Jesus.

15. O Lord, convert every frustration in my life to fulfillment in the name of Jesus.

16. In the name of Jesus, I break the yoke of limitation, stagnation, and failure assigned to keep me far below the level of my ordained prosperity.

17. I break the power of every curse and spirit of delay working against my life and blessings in the name of Jesus.

18. In the name of Jesus, I receive the anointing to prosper and excel and seal my deliverance for prosperity in the blood of Jesus.

19. I rebuke, resist, and overcome every demon assigned to attack the source of my income by the power in the name of Jesus Christ, by the power in the blood of Jesus Christ and by the consuming fire of the Holy Spirit.

20. In the name of Jesus Christ, I decree a release of the wealth of the wicked into the hands of the righteous and receive my share thereof as the Lord apportions.

21. I declare in the name of Jesus that my hands are blessed and that the works of my hands shall prosper.

22. In the name of Jesus, I reverse and cancel every satanic dream designed to steal my prosperity.

CHAPTER SIX

Ministry Crisis

Broadly speaking, ministry refers to the service that the Church is engaged in or pursuing. The work of the ministry refers to the carrying out of ecclesiastical functions, "the washing of feet." The primary work of the ministry is to evangelize for souls and build disciples for Jesus Christ. To accomplish its primary calling, the Ministry will also have to do things incidental to and related to its mission. The church and its individual members are called to do the work of ministry.

The Church Is Faced with a Leadership Crisis

In Ephesians 4, Christ released five ascension gifts to men:

> And he gave some, apostles; and some, prophets; and some evangelists; and some, pastors and teachers; for the perfecting of the saints, for the

work of the ministry, for the edifying of the body of Christ: till we all come in the unity of the faith, and of the knowledge of the Son of God, unto a perfect man, unto the measure of the stature of the fulness of Christ. Ephesians 4:11-13.

Currently, there is a leadership crisis in the church. Many have risen to the offices of apostles, prophets, evangelists, pastors, and teachers that were not appointed by Christ. Like the self-appointed prophetess of Revelation 2:20, Jezebel, some in the body of Christ have assumed titles of authority without being called by Jesus Christ. A person that is not called by Christ is not leading with the Spirit of Christ. Some local churches are infested with false apostles, prophets, evangelists, pastors, and teachers. A false worker in the ministry cannot serve with the Spirit of Christ. He serves with another spirit which is most often a religious spirit or the spirit of mammon. These wicked spirits have been responsible for creating so much distrust, division, distraction, and confusion in the body of Christ. These false ministers, not leading by the Spirit of Christ, eventually adulterate God's holy word to suit their demonic agenda. Some of them are performing false miracles under a satanic anointing and the undiscerning are flocking to them and idolizing them. They in turn, point the undiscerning to their ministry performance instead of leading them to Christ and His finished work on the cross.

For such are false apostles, deceitful workers, transforming themselves into the apostles of Christ. And no marvel; for Satan himself is transformed into an angel of light. Therefore, it is no great thing if his ministers also be transformed as the ministers of righteousness; whose end shall be according to their works. 2 Corinthians 11:13-15.

The leadership crisis in ministry is exacerbated by deception and the inability of many in the body of Christ to test and discern the spirits. Mammon spirits have long hijacked the prosperity gospel and are now seated in the pilot's seat. Jesus Christ will have to come again, this time by the Holy Spirit, and chase these men out of his Father's house. The prosperity gospel that emphasizes prosperity and gives little or no credence to righteousness is being driven by religious spirits and mammon spirits. Every day, unknowing members of the body of Christ are submitting themselves to these spirits by the type of honor they give to their leaders. This is indeed a crisis in ministry that does not seem to be abating.

Mammon spirits invariably manifest greed and manipulation. The ministry leaders operating with these spirits often exhibit an excessive appetite for luxuries and pleasures that merely gratify the flesh. They may claim it is for the advancement of the gospel but these voracious and untamed appetites for expensive and luxurious items have only served to raise questions regarding the authenticity of servants of Christ. They have done more harm than good to the cause of Christ. Such ministry leaders have by their conduct, invited the world to focus on their lavish lifestyles rather than focus on the righteousness of Christ. If Christ called you to lead His people, then you must aspire to be moderate in all things (1Corinthians 9:25; Philippians 4:5).

> All things are lawful unto me, but all things are not expedient: all things are lawful for me, but I will not be brought under the power of any. 1 Corinthians 6:12.

The spirit of Mammon is the spirit of worldliness. All manner of worldliness has found its way into the church. The world culture is prevalent in many local churches. There is a form of godliness, but the central figure is missing: God. The worldly spirit is seen in the form of music that many ministries have now adopted as praise and worship songs. With this crisis in leadership, many leaders that are expected to be the gatekeepers guarding the sheep from the wolves have opened the floodgates for the wolves to come and plunder God's sheep.

The Preeminence of Religious Personalities

Jesus Christ, is the founder and bridegroom of the Church. Jesus Christ must always be the center figure of the Church of God. Jesus, and not a pastor, is the head of the Church. The pastor or minister is just a conduit that Jesus Christ uses to feed His flock. Pastors and other ministers (apostles, prophets, evangelists, missionaries, etc.) must move out of the way for Christ to do what He wants to do.

Many local churches have elevated the Pastor or Man of God to a position ahead of Christ. The star of the church or ministry has become some personality other than Jesus Christ. So much honor is given to the man of God in some Christian circles, that his word is not weighed on the scale of the Word of God. These men of God are only being set up for a fall if they choose not to humble themselves. The crisis in ministry lies in the fact that some ministries are projecting the image of their leaders more than that of Christ. Their websites and social media pages heap praises and accolades on their ministry leaders and have transformed them into celebrities. Though they still preach Christ, the general population sees them instead of Christ. They have made themselves more popular than Christ. This, unfortunately, has caused many to go to a church, ministry, or leader for salvation instead of going to Jesus Christ, the only Savior of the world. They have taken the focus from Christ and put it upon themselves. This also seemed to be a problem in the time of the Apostle Paul. In his epistle to the church in Philippi, Paul states:

> Beware of dogs, beware of evil workers, beware of the concision. For we are the circumcision, which worship God in the spirit, and rejoice in Christ Jesus, and have no confidence in the flesh. Philippians 3:2-3.

Believers in Christ must not put their confidence in a man. Woe is he that puts his trust in a man. Apostle Paul had to also admonish the church in Corinth:

> That your faith should not stand in the wisdom of men, but in the power of God. 1 Corinthians 2:5.

For while one saith, I am of Paul; and another, I am of Apollos; are ye not carnal? Who then is Paul, and who is Apollos, but ministers by whom ye believed, even as the Lord gave to every man? 1 Corinthians 3:4-5.

Well-meaning Christians must pray that the unsaved and unchurched peoples are constantly shown a church where Christ, and not a man, is at the center.

The Ministries of Jezebel and Delilah

Queen Jezebel was the wife of King Ahab of Israel. She, being a very controlling and manipulative person, usurped King Ahab's authority and made decisions in his place. In 1 Kings 21, Jezebel acts for Ahab and forcefully acquired Naboth's vineyard and killed him. Jezebel influenced Ahab to worship Baal and Asherah (1 Kings 16:29-33). Jezebel oppressed and murdered the Lord's prophets. The ministry of Jezebel is rooted in attacking genuine prophetic voices and supplanting them with false prophecy. In Revelation 2:20, Jesus takes a firm stand against Jezebel, "who calls herself a prophetess and is teaching and seducing my servants to practice sexual immorality and to eat food sacrificed to idols."

In a church where the pastor is not the one leading by the Spirit and someone else is in charge via manipulation and intimidation, the latter has most likely usurped the pastor's authority. That person is a Jezebel in the ministry and must be gotten rid of. Christ warns that Jezebel must not be tolerated in his church. Jezebel is a false prophet and teacher, full of cunning and witchcraft manipulation and often seeks to develop a following of her own, especially among those who are discontented or in rebellion. Jezebel will use fake prophecy to manipulate people in the body of Christ. In Christian ministry, too many people are prophesying and yet are under no authority. Many with the help of a Jezebel spirit have released demonic prophecies that have defiled the body of Christ. As Christians, we must plead the blood of Jesus to wash away all defilement of Jezebel spirits operating in our ministries.

The anointing of Jehu is needed in these end times to release the church from the oppressive influence of Jezebel. God raised up Army commander, Jehu to kill Jezebel and destroy the house of Ahab. Ahab, being weak, was fond of using the strength of Jezebel to fight his battles. Ahab is a Jezebel enabler. Therefore, Christ warned the church in Thyatira not to tolerate (enable) Jezebel. For the church to come out of the crisis perpetuated by Jezebel spirits, spiritual warriors will need to rise up in fasting and prayer and bind and cast out this spirit from their environment in the name of Jesus Christ.

Also, inside Christian ministry is the spirit of Delilah. This is the spirit of sexual perversion, seduction, and betrayal. This spirit traps Christian leaders in sexual sin with the main purpose of exposing them and discrediting their ministry. This is what Delilah did to Samson. She drained him of his spiritual and physical strength until he was too weak to confront his enemies. The aim here is not to present a laundry list of the sins in ministry. Rather, the aim here is to raise an alarm because many Christian ministries are in crisis and we must make sure that the gates of hell do not prevail.

With the Delilah spirit comes seduction, sexual perversion, betrayal, and manipulation. Studies have shown an alarming rate of sexual promiscuity among Christians. Many that profess Christ are engaging in pornography, fornication, lesbianism, homosexuality, lusts, and all other forms of sexual perversion. The word of God tells us to flee fornication. Christian ministry must never tolerate this sin which the Bible describes as a sin against one's own body (1 Corinthians 6:18-19). Yet, Delilah subtly comes to propagate this sin in the body of Christ. Delilah, being a seductress and a seducing spirit, has promoted strange fashion styles, music, and dancing in the house of God. Women and men now dress provocatively in the house of God. Many are dressing to seduce the opposite sex.

> In like manner also, that women adorn themselves in modest apparel, with shamefacedness and sobriety; not with broided hair, or gold, or pearls, or costly array. But (which becometh women professing godliness) with good works. 1 Timothy 2:9-10.

However, Delilah's main agenda is to pull down the man of God that occupies a position of authority in God's house. Delilah is good at seeking attention and loves to be noticed. She will pretend that she is genuinely concerned about her victim but is merely setting him up for a fall.

Leaders must learn to test the spirits and the spiritual climates that they minister under.

Lukewarmness in Spiritual Warfare and Deliverance

The terrible powers that are waging war against the church are such that will be defeated through prayer and fasting (Matthew17:21). To engage and defeat principalities and powers, rulers of the darkness of this world, and spiritual wickedness in high places, the church must repent and go back to a lifestyle of prayer and fasting. The gates of hell cannot prevail against a united church that is walking in holiness. Many believers need to be trained on how to pray and to fast. Many believers in the church need to experience the baptism of the Holy Spirit with the evidence of speaking in tongues. Believers need to be strong in the Lord and in the power of His might. Believers need to be conscious of the whole armor of God and make use of it daily.

The lack of awareness regarding the need for spiritual warfare and deliverance is primarily caused by inadequate teaching in the churches. More focus has been placed on prosperity at the expense of the souls of the believers. Many believers and ministers in the body of Christ are not knowledgeable when it comes to spiritual warfare and deliverance. The devil has robbed them for decades and they have done very little to confront the hosts of darkness and appropriate Christ's victory on the cross for their benefit. Leaders in ministry can no longer afford to shy away from teaching the whole counsel of God. The whole truth must be revealed in teaching. A major part of Christ's ministry consisted in healing and deliverance.

One erroneous teaching in the body of Christ that has given devils the upper hand in spiritual warfare is the notion that a Christian cannot have a demon or be demonized. Their reasoning has been that since a Christian has the Holy Spirit dwelling in him, no other spirit can dwell in him. Such a teaching may sound logical and reasonable, but it is not supported by Scripture. This reasoning does not take into consideration that in the Gospels, Jesus delivered believers of demons.

In addition, man is a tripartite being consisting of body, soul, and spirit. The believer's spirit is sealed with the Holy Spirit (2 Corinthians 1:22) and is a no go zone for demons. However, the believer's soul is the seat of his mind, intellect, and emotions. Many believers have not surrendered their minds and emotions to Christ and so demonic powers may afflict them in this area. There are many Christians that are not walking in the mind of Christ and so their minds are targets for all kinds of demonic forces. Rather than confront this phenomenon, many ministries have sought to refer the victims of demonic attacks to Christian psychiatrists and psychologists, who often, merely put a band aid on a deep wound.

The Second Coming of Christ

Christ is the head of the Church. The Church is the body of Christ. Christ is the bridegroom and the Church is the bride of Christ. Christ, being holy, is coming back for a Church without spot, wrinkle, or blemish. Is today's Church prepared to receive Christ when he comes as a thief in the night? Has today's Church like the church in Ephesus (Revelation 2) abandoned her first love and gone in pursuit of other things that have lesser eternal significance? In Revelation 2 and Revelation 3, Jesus Christ visits the seven churches and only two were above reproach. The other five were in crisis and Christ encouraged them to overcome their sins, trials, and distresses in order to inherit the wonderful blessings of he that overcomes. To the lukewarm church of Laodecia, Christ informs them that their riches have become an obstacle to their spiritual life.

> Then shall the kingdom of heaven be likened unto ten virgins, which took their lamps, and went forth to meet the bridegroom. [2] And five of them were wise, and five were foolish. [3] They that were foolish took their lamps, and took no oil with them: [4] But the wise took oil in their vessels with their lamps. [5] While the bridegroom tarried, they all slumbered and slept. [6] And at midnight there was a cry made, Behold, the bridegroom cometh; go ye out to meet him. [7] Then all those virgins arose, and trimmed their lamps. [8] And the foolish said unto the wise, Give us of your oil; for our lamps are gone out. [9] But the wise answered, saying, Not so; lest there be not enough for us and you: but go ye rather to them that sell, and buy for yourselves. [10] And while they went to buy, the bridegroom came; and they

that were ready went in with him to the marriage: and the door was shut. [11] Afterward came also the other virgins, saying, Lord, Lord, open to us. [12] But he answered and said, Verily I say unto you, I know you not.[13] Watch therefore, for ye know neither the day nor the hour wherein the Son of man cometh. Matthew 25:1-13.

The churches, unlike the five foolish virgins, must be positioned at the right place spiritually to receive the Bridegroom. Local churches cannot be "at the market place purchasing oil" at the second coming of Christ. There is an urgency in this hour and the Church as the bride must take heed to what the Spirit is saying and make herself ready to receive the Bridegroom.

Church Growth

There is an apathy toward the things of God in these last days. There is an increased interest among the people in things of the occult. Believers in Christ are getting less involved in church and seem rather content in following a preacher or a service on social media without any involvement or commitment.

This know also, that in the last days perilous times shall come. [2] For men shall be lovers of their own selves, covetous, boasters, proud, blasphemers, disobedient to parents, unthankful, unholy, [3] Without natural affection, trucebreakers, false accusers, incontinent, fierce, despisers of those that are good, [4] Traitors, heady, highminded, lovers of pleasures more than lovers of God; [5] Having a form of godliness, but denying the power thereof: from such turn away. ⁶ For of this sort are they which creep into houses, and lead captive silly women laden with sins, led away with divers lusts, ⁷ Ever learning, and never able to come to the knowledge of the truth. 2 Timothy 3:1-6.

The heart of man in these last days is far removed from God's righteousness. Many believers are falling away from the church. Many yet, are in powerless churches: churches that have a form of godliness but deny the power thereof. Evangelism and soul winning appear to have moved to the internet, digital phase and so many converts are staying within internet, digital boundaries and are not experiencing Christian life of fellowship in a local body.

The reputation of our churches need to be enhanced by reformation and revival. People need to see the presence, the glory, and the power of God once again in the local church. To arrest the decline in church growth, the church must embark on seeking the face of God and crying out for a revival. Jesus mentioned that his house shall be called a house of prayer and not a den of thieves (Matthew 21:13). Prayerlessness, and consequently, powerlessness, have caused stagnation in church growth. The church is meant to be a place where the power of God resides with evidence of signs, miracles, and wonders. Man's wisdom cannot grow the church. The preaching of the true gospel in the power of the Holy Spirit, demonstrated by wonders and signs, is needed to grow the Church (Acts 2:41-43).

Ministries will experience church growth as they begin to view ministry outside of their four walls. The church grows when it takes the gospel of Christ to the ends of the earth. The problem in some churches is that the believers have been led to see the church as existing solely to meet their needs. Christ does not intend for the church to be merely needs driven. Rather, Christ set up the Church to confront the gates of hell and to perfect the saints for their calling. There is the urgent need to recruit more soldiers for Jesus Christ and to disciple them in the Church and not solely on social media. Many of the workers needed to grow the church are reluctant to give their commitment to the local church. They do not want to be under any form of authority and they selfishly desire to be part of this new breed of freelance Christians that is gradually evolving.

> Then saith he unto his disciples, The harvest truly is plenteous, but the laborers are few. Pray ye therefore the Lord of the harvest, that he will send forth laborers into the harvest. Matthew 9:37-38.

It will take praying to the Lord of the harvest, Jesus Christ to bring in and send forth the laborers that are needed for the advancement of the Kingdom of God. Church growth will be meaningless if the people just sat in a big cathedral or auditorium and were never sent forth into the harvest field to bring in the harvest. In these end times, genuine workers for Christ are needed to fish for men and build disciples for Christ.

Persecution of Christians

Christians and the Church of Christ are facing severe persecution in various areas of the world. Persecution of Christians is most severe and continues to rise in Moslem areas such as Saudi Arabia, Iran, Iraq, Yemen, Pakistan, Syria, Northern Nigeria, Somalia, Sudan, Indonesia, and Afghanistan. Persecution of Christians is also intense in non-Moslem states such as North Korea, China, Russia, and Myanmar (Burma).

Yea, and all that will live godly in Christ Jesus shall suffer persecution. 2 Timothy 3:12.

Then shall they deliver you up to be afflicted, and shall kill you: and ye shall be hated of all nations for my name's sake. Matthew 24:9.

Remember the word that I have said unto you, The servant is not greater than his lord. If they have persecuted me, they will also persecute you; if they have kept my saying, they will keep yours also. John 15:20.

They shall put you out of the synagogues: yea, the time cometh, that whosoever killeth you will think that he doeth God service. John 16:2.

One of the most dangerous places to be a Christian is in North Korea where the government sees any influx of Christianity as a form of westernization. Islamic extremism as propagated by organizations like ISIS, Al-Qaeda, Hezbollah, and Boko Haram seems to be the driving force responsible for the most severe and widespread persecution of Christians.

The crisis here is worsened by the apathy of many Christians and churches toward the fate of their fellow believers in territories that encourage the persecution of Christians solely because of their faith in Christ. The churches, especially in the affluent West, must not only be in prayer for the Lord's keeping power over persecuted Christians but must also share more of their resources with them. We must pray for more of God's grace to strengthen them in their trials so that they do not compromise because of fear and threatening from their persecutors. Churches that are currently free from persecution must not assume that they are immune from future persecution. The spread of persecution is a sign of Christ's imminent return.

As the true Church of Christ continues to take a rigid stand for righteousness in liberal democratic societies, it will face animosity from a frustrated public that believes that the removing of moral restraints ensures the happiness of everyone. Righteousness exalts a nation, sin is the reproach of a people (Proverbs 14:34). As sin further degrades the moral, social, political, and economic fabric of popular cultures, Christians will be viewed as a problem. Sinners tend to find solace with those that approve of their sins (Romans 1:32) and the silent hostility against Christianity will most likely evolve into an active one.

Christians in government and high positions of authority can no longer afford to be complacent. Queen

Esther sought to be silent when her people were being persecuted under the reign of King Artaxerxes. Esther probably felt that being in the palace would give her protection from the planned persecution against the Jews. She was dragging her feet and saying that she could not approach the king until she was invited into his presence. Then Queen Esther's uncle, Mordecai sent Esther this reply which is very instructive for well to do churches today:

> Then Mordecai commanded to answer Esther, Think not with thyself that thou shalt escape in the king's house, more than all the Jews. For if thou altogether holdest thy peace at this time, then shall there enlargement and deliverance arise to the Jews from another place; but thou and thy father's house shall be destroyed: and who knoweth whether thou art come to the kingdom for such a time as this? Esther 4:13-14.

The entire body of Christ worldwide must respond to the persecution of Christians with one voice. Pressure must be exerted on democratic governments which support tyrannical governments that endorse persecution of Christians in their territory. Last century, pressure in forms of economic sanctions were imposed on the white minority racist regime in South Africa that pursued a policy of apartheid. The same can be done for countries whose governments endorse the torture and murder of innocent lives merely because of their faith. Just like Mordecai advised Queen Esther, so also, the body of Christ cannot afford to be complacent.

Blessed are they which are persecuted for righteousness' sake: for theirs is the kingdom of heaven. Blessed are ye, when men shall revile you, and persecute you, and shall say all manner of evil against you falsely, for my sake. Rejoice, and be exceeding glad: for great is your reward in heaven: for so persecuted they the prophets which were before you. Matthew 5:10-12.

Prayers for Stronger Ministries in Christ

1. Heavenly Father, I bring the body of Christ before You and ask for unity and love to grow in the midst thereof.

2. In the name of Jesus Christ, Holy Spirit sweep through the churches and expose and remove leaders that are not submitted to the Word of God.

3. Holy Spirit convict ministry leaders and workers that convert God's glory to their glory, in the name of Jesus.

4. Heavenly Father, purge the churches of worldliness and sin and bring revival fire to our churches in the mighty name of Jesus Christ.

5. In the name of Jesus Christ, let every gospel that does not seek first the kingdom of God and His righteousness die out.

6. Holy Spirit raise up more genuine leaders to disciple believers in Christ in the name of Jesus.

7. I come against every spirit of lukewarmness in my local church in the mighty name of Jesus.

8. Heavenly Father, in the name of Jesus, orchestrate the disgrace and downfall of spirits of lukewarmness that have paralyzed the drive for evangelism, spiritual warfare, prayers, and deliverance in our churches.

9. Holy Spirit expose every false doctrine that is being preached in churches that the people will not be deceived in the name of Jesus.

10. Lord Jesus Christ, baptize the churches with a spirit of tarrying and travailing in prayer.

11. Lord Jesus, I pray that You raise up and send forth laborers to bring in a harvest of souls in these last days.

12. Heavenly Father, place a burden for souls on the Church in the name of Jesus.

13. Heavenly Father, touch the hearts of fellow Christians to support persecuted Christians all over the world in Jesus' name.

14. In the name of Jesus, Lord touch the heart of persecutors of Christians that they too will come to a saving knowledge of Jesus Christ.

15. Heavenly Father, in the name of Jesus Christ, strengthen persecuted Christians and their families all over the world that they will not compromise or give up their faith.

16. I pray for boldness, wisdom, courage, and support for persecuted Christians in the name of Jesus.

17. In the name of Jesus, Father send more angels to protect unarmed and helpless believers in Christ from violent attacks by Islamic extremists.

18. Lord, keep us believers rapture ready for Your second coming.

CHAPTER SEVEN

Defeating Your Crisis

Overcoming crisis is not for the slothful nor the unwise. Focus, research (diligently seeking), hard work, among other things, are required. The crisis must first be defeated in your mind. You must have the faith that as you command the mountains to be removed and cast into the sea that it shall be as you have said. The battle is first won in the mind. You cannot afford to be double-minded. In a crisis, you must have the right reactions. How you react is very important. Crisis will often provoke you to react in panic, anxiety, fear, jealousy, anger, and other emotions. You must learn to rest on the peace of Christ and be still (Psalm 46:10). Yet, you must know when to take appropriate action and how to react.

In this I labor, striving according to His power, which effectively works in me. Colossians 1:29, MEV.

As you work your way out of a crisis, you must ask God for His power, wisdom, and grace. Your connection to God is of utmost importance. "The steps of a good man are ordered by the Lord: and he delighted in his way." (Psalm 27:23). Coming out of crisis is a step by step process. In the wilderness, the children of Israel refused to hearken to the Lord, and the Lord ordered their steps to wander in the wilderness for forty years. You must listen to God and do it God's way so that a journey of 7 days does not end up becoming a crisis of 40 years.

> Not as though I had already attained, either were already perfect: but I follow after, if that I may apprehend that for which also I am apprehended of Christ Jesus. Brethren, I count not myself to have apprehended: but this one thing I do, forgetting those things which are behind, and reaching forth unto those things which are before, I press toward the mark for the prize of the high calling of God in Christ Jesus. Philippians 3:12-14.

The Scripture quoted above is speaking with respect to trials and hardships. Apostle Paul is saying here that when faced with challenging times, there is one thing he does and that is, he presses on. The way he accomplishes this is by first forgetting what is behind (the past) and straining toward what is ahead (the present and the future). Whenever you are in a severe time of testing, one thing you want to do is to first disentangle yourself from the poisons and traumas of the past. You will keep what you have learned from the past so that you do not repeat the same mistakes again. In a trial, the present is often littered with loss, pain, betrayal, and insecurities that threaten to accompany the person into his future. The essential point is not to dwell in this dark area but to move forward, to press on. Read Philippians 3:12-14 one more time. It says what is ahead (the future, the promise) requires effort ("reaching forth"). Every crisis, has a promise at its end. It is your straining toward what is ahead that requires you to keep faith and persevere. Satan will like to keep you focused on the past and your current circumstances so that you do not fight hard for your wonderful promises located in the future. Learn from the past and move forward.

Jesus also demonstrated this principle in Luke 9:59-60:

> And he said unto another, Follow me. But he said, Lord, suffer me first to go and bury my father. Jesus said unto him, Let the dead bury their dead: but go thou and preach the kingdom of God.

This man had work cut out for him in the present and future, but was looking back at issues that were dead and in the past. Jesus did not allow this man to use his circumstances located in the past as an excuse to avoid a present call. Until you break the chains tying you to the past, it will be difficult to accomplish that which God is calling you for.

When you are going through a particularly difficult time and all hell seems to have broken loose and there is nowhere to turn to, look up unto Jesus Christ alone, the author and finisher of faith. You must turn and yield completely to the Lord Jesus Christ. Jesus committed no sin and, yet he endured the greatest agony for our sakes.

To defeat your crisis, you must appreciate that your crisis has come into your life at this time for a reason. Do not be bitter with a crisis, rather, learn from it. The crisis is designed to take you to your promise and so, the right approach is very important.

What Do You Do in a Crisis to Provoke the Hand of God to Move in Your Favor?

1. Repentance

> Behold, the Lord's hand is not shortened, that it cannot save; neither his ear heavy, that it cannot hear. But your iniquities have separated between you and your God, and your sins have hid his face from you, that he will not hear. Isaiah 59:1-2.

Repentance opens the door for new beginnings and new possibilities. You must repent of everything that causes God to turn his face away from you. Repentance requires more than just changing or merely being sorry. You must repent of those negative things that may have led you into a crisis. You cannot keep doing those negative things and expect to come out of your crisis. You cannot keep doing any wrong thing that you are doing and expect a good outcome. When you continue in the same line of conduct or attitude, it is an indication that you have not genuinely repented. In your crisis, you want to draw closer to God and this always begins with repentance. Repent of any secret sin or open sin and be determined in your heart not to honor that sin or repeat that sin.

2. Forgiveness

The will of God is that you forgive others, forgive yourself and ask God for forgiveness. Unforgiveness generates bitterness in the heart and when you forgive, the spirit of bitterness loses the ground it had to remain in your heart.

If you keep unforgiveness in your heart, Satan will have a legal right to torment you in your crisis. In Matthew 18:23-34, Jesus tells the parable of a servant that was forgiven much by his master and yet, refused to forgive a fellow servant of little. This unforgiving servant incurred his master's wrath and was handed over to the tormentors to be tortured until he paid back all that he owed. You cannot receive deliverance from the Lord until you forgive all that have offended you. Your forgiving others, strips Satan of his advantage over you. Your refusing to forgive those that offended you gives Satan ammunition to use against you. Do not prolong your crisis by holding on to malice, bitterness, resentment, and anger toward anyone that has offended you. Without your giving and receiving forgiveness, you will be fighting a battle against forces of darkness that you will never win. A stalemate in a crisis is not victory. Forgiveness brings you closer to the things that God has in store for you.

3. Praise

Ask the Lord to deposit songs of praises in your heart. In times of crisis, you must praise your way through. You cannot afford not to have a song of praise in your heart. Proverbs 15:13 states that a happy heart makes the face cheerful, but heartache crushes the spirit. Songs of joy and victory offered to God in praise will lift your spirit up because God inhabits the praises of His people (Psalm 22:3).

There was a time in my life when I lost almost everything. I was homeless, unemployed, in deportation proceedings, and in a health crisis among other things. In this time of severe testing, I would sing to the Lord everywhere I went. I would sing to the Lord as I walked on the streets of Brooklyn, New York and the Bronx, New York. I would sing to the Lord in the train stations and on the trains, and in my tiny room that I was able to later afford. As I made a joyful noise unto the Lord, I could truly sense that the joy of the Lord was my strength (Nehemiah 8:10).

When you wake up in the morning, begin your day by praising God. In the spirit realm, your praise has the effect of weakening the enemy's strongholds over you. In 2 Chronicles 2:20, as the Israelites sang and praised God, God Himself, set ambushes against their enemies and gave Israel the promised victory through King Jehoshaphat. Your praise will move the power of God to fight against your spiritual enemies that are determined to detain you in your crisis and see you live in frustration.

A heart that praises God will have no room for grumbling, murmuring, and complaining. Complaining comes from a sour heart that refuses to see the good that God is working out in a crisis. Complaining is a means of saying to God that God does not know what He is doing or that you do not believe in or approve of what God is doing. Every crisis has a promise and the effect of complaining is to remove you from the promise. A complaining heart is evidence of unbelief. If you believe, you will wait patiently for the promise. The Israelites that complained in the wilderness never entered Canaan, the land of promise.

4. Thanksgiving

Whatever you may be going through, you must cultivate and maintain a heart of gratitude. If care is not taken, it is easy for one to become unthankful. God looks at the heart. When in a crisis, we tend to be anxious for a solution. In the 100th Psalm, the Bible admonishes us to enter God's gates with thanksgiving and to come into His courts with praise.

> Be careful for nothing; but in everything by prayer and supplication with thanksgiving let your requests be made known unto God. And the peace of God, which passeth all understanding, shall keep your hearts and minds through Christ Jesus. Philippians 4:6-7.

> In everything give thanks: for this is the will of God in Christ Jesus concerning you. 1 Thessalonians 5:18.

No matter the circumstances, thank God. Thank God for everything and thank God in everything. Do not grumble. Do not complain. Thank God and praise Him.

5. The Word

Every day and more so in tough times, you need to read, study, meditate, and memorize the Word of God. Ephesians 6:17 describes the Word of God as the sword of the Spirit. It is not your sword; it is the Holy Spirit's sword. As you use and apply the Word of God, the Holy Spirit takes it and fights with it on your behalf. Hebrews 4:12 refers to the Word of God as living and active and sharper than any double-edged sword. The Word penetrates to even dividing soul and spirit, joints, and marrow; it judges the thoughts and attitudes of the heart. The Word of God is an offensive weapon against the hosts of darkness. Attack is the best form of defense. You must know the Word of God. You must know the Holy Bible like you never did before. After 40 days of fasting in the wilderness, Jesus defeated Satan in battle by challenging him with the written Word of God (Matthew 4:1-11).

In heaven, the blood of Jesus Christ and the word of the testimony of the saints overcame Satan (Revelation 12:11). The more you know, obey, and apply the Word of God, the sharper will be the sword of the Holy Spirit fighting for you. The Word makes it clear that the blood of Jesus overcame Satan and that when God sees the blood, He ensures that the angels of destruction passes over His people. The more you know these truths from the Word, the more you can fire them against the enemy in battle. Remember that the consumption of the Word of God generates and grows faith in your spirit. In Romans 10:17, we read that: "So then faith cometh by hearing, and hearing by the word of God."

6. Worship

Worship is total submission, reliance, and exclusive adoration in reverence to God. God is spirit, and his worshipers must worship in spirit and in truth (John 4:24). In times of crisis, there are many who run from pillar to post and helter-skelter. Their panic is evidence of a lack of trust in the One they profess to worship. Do not panic. Rather, seek help from the right source and not from your enemy's camp. When out of frustration and the need for quick answers or revelation, you walk into the enemy's camp to seek help, you are making your situation worse.

> For such are false apostles, deceitful workers, transforming themselves into the apostles of Christ. And no marvel; for Satan himself is transformed into an angel of light. Therefore it is no great thing if his ministers also be transformed as the ministers of righteousness; whose end shall be according to their works. 2 Corinthians 11:13-15.

Be careful when searching for spiritual help. Make sure you consult from the kingdom of light. Darkness often tries to masquerade as light. God is very interested in who you consult. If you consult a servant of darkness, you are indirectly submitting to his god. You are in essence bowing down to and worshiping his god. The only true and living God is a jealous God and He does not take the worship that is due Him lightly. Jesus said that it is impossible to serve two masters; you either love one and despise the other or vice versa. In these times, you cannot afford to live a double life. Living a double life makes a mockery of your worship of God. You cannot have one foot in and one foot out. Stay in the Ark of safety, the Ark of the Covenant so that you do not perish with the unbelievers. God has revealed Himself in the person of Jesus Christ. Worship God with all your heart, soul, mind, and strength. What fellowship has light with darkness? Do not be yoked together with unbelievers because righteousness and wickedness have nothing in common (2 Corinthians 6:14-15).

7. Fellowship and Counseling

During a trial, you will need to seek godly counsel because you do not have all the answers.

> For by wise counsel thou shalt make thy war: and in the multitude of counsellors is safety. Proverbs 24:6.

In the multitude of counsel is safety. Just be careful that you are listening to the right godly counsel. Do not listen to the voice of a snake like Eve did in the Garden of Eden. Eve probably thought that the snake was a friend. The snake turned out to be a foe. Be careful and ask the Lord to lead and guide you. The Lord will lead you to the right group of believers that can encourage and support you. So long as God is for you, it is not as bad as it seems. Consider David who had to encourage himself in the Lord when all his men were thinking of stoning him to death because of the loss of family and property they suffered in Ziklag at the hands of the Amalekites (1 Samuel 30). In his crisis moment, David inquired of the Lord and the Lord led David to an Egyptian that held the key to his pursuing, overtaking and recovering all that was lost at the invasion of the Amalekites.

8. Prayer

As you praise, thank, and worship God and become built up in His Word, your prayer life will witness a dramatic upsurge. There are some troubles that do not go away except by prayer and fasting. Fasting intensifies the effect of prayer. Prayer is communication to God from the heart.

> Ask, and it shall be given you, seek, and ye shall find; knock, and it shall be opened unto you. For every one that asketh receiveth; and he that seeketh findeth; and to him that knocketh it shall be opened. Matthew 7:7-8.

The above quoted Scripture establishes that the door is not opened (that is, an opportunity) for you in the spirit realm until you start knocking. Also, when you seek, you will find the solution. To receive, you must ask (pray). These are some very wonderful promises given by Jesus Christ who is the Truth, the Way, and the Life. Jesus cannot and can never lie. He said it and, so we know that it is so.

Believe this promise. In prayer, just ask, seek, and knock and Jesus will do the rest. You must pray as if your all and because your all is hanging on that prayer.

The things of God are for those that desire them and that are prepared to let go of everything to get a hold of God. Pray with the attitude of Jacob in Genesis 32:22-30. Here, Jacob wrestled with heaven until he was blessed. Jacob was a man that was determined to forget his wicked past and press on in his present reality unto the promises he received from God. In Genesis 32, Jacob is leaving behind his past of disappointments, fears, and deceit and pressing on to realize the promises of God. This period marked a crisis in the life of Jacob as he was not yet certain how his brother Esau, whom he had defrauded out of his birth right and blessing, would receive him. Yet, Jacob in his determination, wrestled with the angel of God until day break and refused to let the angel of God go until he was blessed (Genesis 32:24-29).

As you pray, ask God to fill you with the Holy Spirit. As you are continually filled with the Spirit, you will not walk in the flesh nor pray in the flesh (Galatians 5:6).

As you live a lifestyle that reflects these eight things listed above, your victory is assured.

Hinderances to Overcoming Crisis

As you are pressing on out of crisis, you must also beware of the devil's devices designed to frustrate you and prolong your crisis. You must absolutely guard against these. Some fiery darts that forces of darkness would try to throw in your way to discourage you from advancing through your crisis into your destiny may include the following:

1. Doubt

> But let him ask in faith, nothing wavering. For he that wavereth is like a wave of the sea driven with the wind and tossed. For let not that man think that he shall receive anything of the Lord. A double minded man is unstable in all his ways. James 1:6-8.

When you petition God in prayer, you must do so in faith. You must not give room for doubt to corrupt your faith. Faith wavers mainly because of doubt, complaining, and fear. A faith that wavers communicates a lack of trust in God to deliver on His promise. Do not be like the waves of the sea that are driven and tossed by the wind. Do not let your faith be influenced by what you see. When you walk by faith and not by sight, your faith will be unwavering. To receive anything of the Lord, you must approach God with unwavering faith and maintain a lifestyle that demonstrates that quality of faith. In Matthew 14, we see Simon Peter walking on the water as he put his trust in Jesus. The moment he began to look at the crisis of the storm, he began to sink. The object of your unwavering faith must be Christ. Jesus tells the story of the persistent widow who despite the discouragement she suffered at the hand of the unrighteous judge maintained an unwavering faith. As a result, the unrighteous judge yielded to the demand of the widow and granted her justice (Luke 18:1-8).

A double minded man is unstable in all his ways. Instability is a hindrance to your spiritual growth. When a person is unstable, he is not trustworthy. No one likes to extend help to people that they cannot trust. Double-mindedness is nurtured in an environment of confusion, doubt, and mistrust and breeds instability. Be single minded: trust in the Lord with all your heart and lean not on your own understanding (Proverbs 3:5).

Am I going to make it? How would I come out of this? These are some of the dangerous questions that the devil and his agents will try to plant in your heart. If you entertain these undesirable elements, your faith will start to diminish. Only believe. Jesus in John 11:40 told the sister of Lazarus, Martha, that if she believed, she would see the glory of God. You need to see the glory of God during and at the end of your trial. This calls for unwavering faith.

And Jesus answering saith unto them, Have faith in God. For verily I say unto you, That whosoever shall say unto this mountain, Be thou removed, and be thou cast into the sea; and shall not doubt in his heart, but shall believe that those things which he saith shall come to pass; he shall have whatsoever he saith. Therefore I say unto you, What things soever ye desire, when ye pray, believe that ye receive them, and ye shall have them. Mark 11:22-24.

Speak the word of God because the word of God has power. Jesus is the Word and the Word will not return to God void. It will accomplish the purpose for which it is sent, for which it was spoken (Isaiah 55:1; John 1:1). The Word of God is Spirit and Life. By praying the word of God and believing it in your heart without doubting, you will have that which you have asked for. God told the prophet Ezekiel to prophesy to the valley of dry bones. In similar fashion, you can speak resurrection power through the word of God and raise up any dead Lazarus in your life that needs to come alive.

You must believe the Word. You must believe in your heart that God wants to bless you. You must know the Word to believe and act on what the Word says. Faith without works is dead. In Mark 11:22-24, Jesus is letting believers know that they need to start calling those things that are not as though they are (Romans 4:17). This is what God did with Abraham. He addressed Abram as Abraham: what he was destined to be – the father of many nations. Speak the Word! Do not repeat or embrace negative words. For the power of God to cause something that God has promised (for example, prosperity, healing, deliverance) to be manifested in this natural realm, you must speak or confess God's word and agree with God without any iota of doubt. Then God will back up His promise by bringing it to pass in the natural realm. Remember, God created all things and, so He can change anything. With God, nothing is impossible (Luke 1:37).

2. Fear

> For God hath not given us the spirit of fear, but of power, and of love, and of a sound mind. 2 Timothy 1:7

As a believer, God calls you to operate in the spirit that he has given unto you: the spirit of power, love, and of a sound mind. When a believer operates in fear, he is in bondage. Fear is an indication of demonic presence in the life of a believer. The spirit of fear does not come from God. It is from Satan. A believer that is a coward is one that sees God as a very small God. A very small god is unable to deliver from a big crisis because that god is so limited. Do not limit God to your capacity. When you see God for Who He truly is, you will not live in cowardice.

The devil uses the spirit and instruments of fear to intimidate the believer from taking the necessary action that is needed to move forward into his destiny. If fear envelops you, you will find it difficult to do that which God has called you to do or to go where God has ordained for you to go. The army of Israel was paralyzed by fear when the champion of the Philistines, Goliath challenged them. The Israelite army kept looking at the source of their fear, Goliath. So long as they focused on the size and strength of Goliath, they saw their own weaknesses and could not be delivered from what seemed to be a major crisis before them. But David was different. He did not look at the size or strength of Goliath. David's reference point was always the Lord. God had delivered him in the past, and so he was

not intimidated by a giant called Goliath. David understood that God was bigger than any giant that will ever
face him, including the giant of fear. David focused on the
omnipotent God rather than the giant of intimidation.

Furthermore, it is quite intimidating to walk on water.
Simon Peter learnt that so long as he kept his focus on
Jesus, he walked on the water but that as soon as he began
looking at the water, he began to sink. You overcome fear
by leaning on Jesus and by confronting it. You do not run
away from fear. You confront fear in the name of the Lord.
Running away in itself, suggests that it was the fear that
pursued you. Do not let the enemy use fear as a weapon
to intimidate you and keep you from doing that which is
necessary for your advancement.

3. Murmuring and Complaining

> Wherein ye greatly rejoice, though now for a season,
> if need be, ye are in heaviness through manifold
> temptations: That the trial of your faith, being much
> more precious than of gold that perisheth, though it
> be tried with fire, might be found unto praise and
> honor and glory at the appearing of Jesus Christ.
> 1 Peter 1:6-7

The evidence of your faith is seen in your ability to
greatly rejoice during trials and temptations. True faith
does not breakdown in adversity. Most times, adversity
strengthens faith. The Word of God says that your faith
has more value than gold. Your faith shall be tried to prove
its measure and its value. A trial could be of a short or a

long duration. A trial could be a light or a severe testing. A lengthy trial will examine the perseverance level of your faith. Do you have the type of faith that endures to the end? The trial of faith will also reveal whether you are a double-minded man or a man that stands on God's word no matter what. The faith of Abraham was tested. God promised Abraham a son and Abraham had to wait for years, not wavering in his faith, to see the manifestation of God's promise. Trials mature our faith. Faith that is not tested cannot be trusted.

Furthermore, the trial of your faith should result in praise, honor, and glory at the appearing of Jesus Christ. Your faith must be such that Jesus Christ will commend it. Christ commended the faith of the Roman Centurion, the Canaanite woman, and others that demonstrated exceptional faith amid serious challenges. You must see life's trial's as an opportunity to grow your faith. The Lord expects you to rejoice in your trials. Complaining and murmuring because of a trial is a testimony that your faith is weak. Faith does not complain. Faith is expectant and always looking ahead. Your faith will only bring glory to God if you can endure and rejoice in your trial.

> And when they came to Marah, they could not drink of the waters of Marah, for they were bitter: therefore, the name of it was called Marah. And the people murmured against Moses, saying, What shall we drink? Exodus 15:23-24.

In their journey from Egypt toward Canaan, as the children of Israel journeyed in the wilderness, a place of severe testing, they got to Marah. At Marah, the waters were bitter and undrinkable. Being in the wilderness is extremely harsh and will generally reveal our human weaknesses and failures. It was in such a wilderness that the Israelites stumbled on the bitter waters of Marah. In their thirst, they probably had some initial excitement at the sight of water. The water turned out to be bitter and unfit for human consumption. The Israelites turned their frustration toward Moses and began to murmur against Moses, saying, What shall we drink? The conditions in the wilderness revealed what was in the children of Israel. Tests have a way of revealing what is inside of us. It exposed the unbelief that resided in the hearts of the children of Israel. A few days prior they were praising the Lord for delivering them from Pharaoh's armies and soon after that, they were complaining.

Water is essential to life and provides refreshing. The lack of water in the wilderness became a recurring test of faith for Israel. Unfortunately, they had difficulty trusting the God that miraculously delivered them from Egyptian slavery to provide them with water. When you are faced with a lack, what do you do? Do you complain, or do you trust the Lord that brought you out of captivity? When a person in authority does not meet your expectations, what do you do? Do you complain? Avoid complaining against persons in authority over you as God may view this as a complaint against Him (God) that appointed the authority.

Murmuring tends to incur the wrath of God (Numbers 11; Numbers 16) and terminate destinies. In life's trials and crisis, you must avoid at all costs, the temptation to grumble and murmur. Develop rather, a lifestyle of thanksgiving and praise.

4. Anger

In crisis, the devil wants you to be angry to the point where you put all the blame on God or others, including yourself.

For the wrath of man worketh not the righteousness of God. James 1:20.

The function of a spirit of anger is to distort your perception of reality, especially in your relationships and in a time of testing. If anger is left unattended, it will lead to resentment, lack of control, unforgiveness, and strife among other things. If you are operating in anger and have anger rooted in you, it must be dealt with for you to see your victory in spiritual warfare. You need God's righteousness because human anger does not produce the righteousness that God desires (James 1:20).

The spirit of anger seeks to control a life and will seek for the right opportunity to enter or to manifest in that life. Whenever you feel anger rising in you to cause disaffection with others, do not let anger have its way. Deal with anger. Seek deliverance if that anger is out of control. Many have lost out on a blessing because they manifested anger when they should have been calm. Anger can destroy a marriage, a career, and close doors that ought to be opened. It can make people run away from someone identified as an angry person. Do not let the sun go down on your wrath. Do not let your anger linger. When anger lingers, it opens the door for the devil to exploit your vulnerable state and delay your breakthroughs.

5. Confusion

The antidote to confusion is to pray to God for wisdom, knowledge, and understanding. The devil is a deceiver and uses deception to try and confuse us. We get conflicting messages for the same problem and begin to wonder which is right. Satan may be at work in such a situation. He tries to distort our understanding. If confused, it is best to wait upon the Lord for direction. Meditate on the Word of God for guidance. His Word is a lamp unto our feet and a light for our path. At the proper time, God will order your steps out of any confusion as you continue to trust Him.

> For now we see through a glass, darkly; but then face to face: now I know in part; but then shall I know even as also I am known. 1 Corinthians 13:12.

In a crisis, what you know is often based on imperfect and incomplete knowledge and understanding. You do not have all the answers and, so you will have to operate by faith. You get to see glimpses of what God has promised and there will be some unanswered questions or some unsolved parts of the puzzle. Do not succumb to confusion but rather, trust in God and move forward in faith.

The battle is the Lord's. You are more than a conqueror in Christ Jesus. You are an overcomer in Christ. Any crisis you find yourself in has the potential to usher you into a higher realm of anointing, a higher realm of strength, a higher realm of faith, a higher realm of testimony, and a higher realm of purpose. Whatever the enemy intends for evil, God reverses it and makes it work out for our good. Your victory over crisis is assured. Romans 8:31 declares: "What shall we then say to these things? If God be for us, who can be against us?" No power can stand against God. God is for you so long as you know and abide in His Son, Jesus Christ. You cannot have a testimony without a test. Your testimony in part, is that God is using the trials of life, to make you a new person. God is shaping your character and as you are tried in the fire, you will come forth as pure gold (Job 23:10).

In the battles that are being fought, you cannot afford to be neutral. Stand, no matter what, in Christ and for Christ. Do not concede ground to the enemy no matter how hard and painful it may seem. You will eventually be rewarded with a life that bears witness to the character of Christ.

Prayers to Help in Crisis

1. Heavenly Father, hear my cry for help in the name of Jesus.

2. Heavenly Father, I repent of every anger and bitterness that I have held on to from my past and in my present trials and ask of Your forgiveness in Jesus' name.

3. In the name of Jesus, I forgive all that have sinned against me.

4. Any thing not of God in me or around me, that is feeding crisis in my life, I command you to die, in the name of Jesus.

5. I break all generational and hidden curses of setback, poverty, failure, and rejection in the mighty name of Jesus Christ.

6. Lord Jesus Christ, baptize me with the Holy Spirit and Fire, I pray. O Lord, let there be through the baptism of the Holy Spirit, a rapid manifestation of deliverance and victory in my life in the mighty name of Jesus Christ.

7. In the name of Jesus, I reverse the pronouncements and incantations of darkness upon my life.

8. I refuse to be controlled, remotely or otherwise, by any evil power in the name of Jesus Christ.

9. Every power denying the manifestation of God's prophecy for my life and in my ministry, O God of Elijah, scatter them and destroy their works against me in the mighty name of Jesus.

10. Heavenly Father, let my victory over powers and rulers of darkness be sealed in the blood of Jesus Christ.

11. Every deeply entrenched problem in my life, bred by curses and evil incantations, dry to the roots and be destroyed in the name of Jesus.

12. I bind every strong man delegated to hinder my progress and command all the adversaries of my breakthroughs to scatter and be put to shame in the name of Jesus.

13. I bind every strong man holding my privileges, rights, and finances captive in the name of Jesus.

14. I bind and render impotent the spirit of marginal and minimal success and limitation, in the mighty name of Jesus.

15. Lord, entrench my matter into the mind of those that will assist me so that they will not be distracted by the enemy, in the name of Jesus.

16. Heavenly Father, anoint me with the spirit of wisdom, knowledge, understanding, and discernment in the name of Jesus.

17. Heavenly Father, in the name of Jesus Christ, let praise and thanksgiving never depart from my heart.

18. O Lord, give me the grace to maintain my integrity in my life's trials in the name of Jesus.

Other Books by
Apostle Idemudia Guobadia

Fighting for Deliverance
Deeper Dimensions of Power
I Never Stopped Believing
Working for Christ

Available at Amazon.com

FIGHTING FOR DELIVERANCE

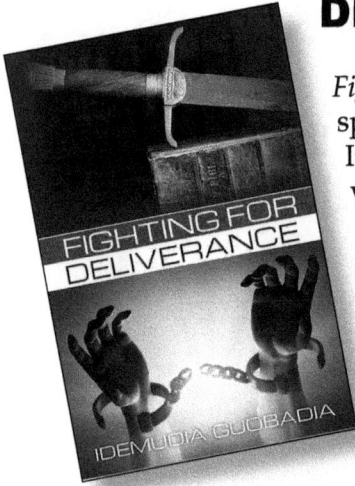

Fighting for Deliverance is a book on spiritual warfare and deliverance. It demonstrates how to get the victory in casting out demons and by binding powers of darkness. It teaches people how powers of darkness exploit their weaknesses in order to maintain an upper hand against them. By exposing the devices of Satan, people in need of deliverance are presented with spiritual strategies required to fight for and maintain their deliverance from demonic oppression.

Available at Amazon.com

DEEPER DIMENSIONS OF POWER

Deeper Dimensions of Power discusses the various levels of power in the spirit realm and how you can connect to the highest of all powers which is, the Source of all power. There is a reason today why many Christians are not walking in power and victory. There is a reason why many are Christians and yet are not overcomers in Christ. One reason is because they have not learned how to disconnect from toxic mindsets and truly connect to Christ. *Deeper Dimensions of Power* teaches you how to walk in your authority and power as a believer. To influence and command your environment, you will need to know how to flow in the Holy Spirit. Until you demonstrate superior power against the forces of darkness and destroy their cause, you will remain where you are. In *Deeper Dimensions of Power,* you will see that the superior power of Christ is available to you if you are willing to pay the price.

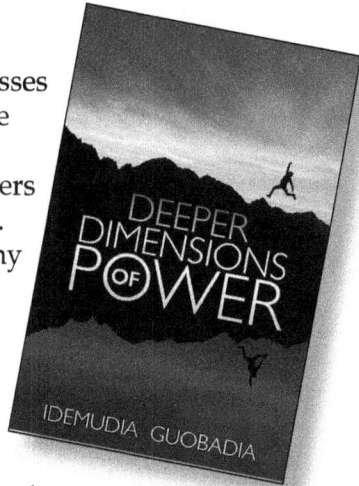

Available at Amazon.com

I NEVER STOPPED BELIEVING

I Never Stopped Believing is an inspirational book that attests to the power of Christ to set people and nations free from demonic powers of darkness. While discussing general problems and accomplishments of humanity, it focuses on the spiritual dimensions of the human dilemma. The author uses his testimony of being delivered from the power of the occult through the intervention of Jesus Christ to encourage others that there is hope in Christ.

Available at Amazon.com

WORKING FOR CHRIST

Working for Christ challenges the believer to do work that Christ would recognize and commend. It shows that work, no matter how good, that is done outside of Christ is no value in the kingdom of God. Until you work in Christ, you have not worked for Christ. The worker for Christ must be kingdom minded ready to wage spiritual warfare and to intercede as often as the Spirit of Christ demands. There is so much work to be done and Christ is looking for committed workers! This book is written to show you how to make your work for God count.

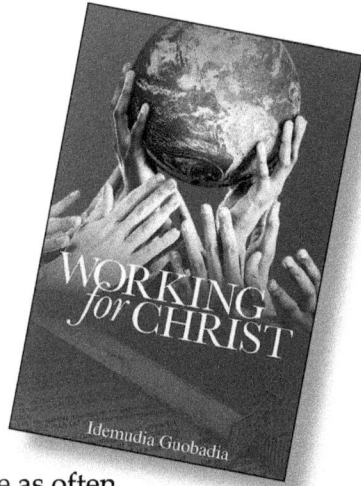

Available at Amazon.com

www.ingramcontent.com/pod-product-compliance
Lightning Source LLC
Chambersburg PA
CBHW072012040426
42447CB00009B/1605